CLEAR TEACHING:

With Direct Instruction, Siegfried Engelmann Discovered a Better Way of Teaching

By Shepard Barbash

About the Author

Shepard Barbash has been a writer for thirty years. His work has appeared in *The New York Times*, *Wall Street Journal*, *Washington Post*, *Smithsonian Magazine*, *City Journal*, *Education Next* and other publications. He is former bureau chief of the *Houston Chronicle* in Mexico City and is the author of four published books. As a volunteer he has advised the Georgia Governor's Office and the Atlanta Public Schools on curricular issues and has organized teacher training programs and written grants for APS. He has also worked for E.D. Hirsch at the Core Knowledge Foundation.

All photos provided courtesy of the Association for Direct Instruction. We gratefully acknowledge their contribution.

TABLE OF CONTENTS

Clear Teaching

Appendices

FOREWORD
by J.E. Stone, Ed.D.

Closing America's Achievement Gap:
A Powerful Tool is Being Ignored

History shows that innovations with obvious benefits are often ignored and resisted for decades or even centuries. Take the case of citrus fruit as a treatment for scurvy.

Prior to 1750, scurvy was a horrific problem on long sea voyages. As author Jonathan Lamb notes, "In 1499, Vasco da Gama lost 116 of his crew of 170; in 1520, Magellan lost 208 out of 230... all mainly to scurvy."

You would think that any promising treatment would be readily adopted—but it wasn't.

In a 1601 voyage from England to India, British captain James Lancaster gave three teaspoons of lemon juice per day to the sailors on his flagship. The crews of the other three ships under his command received none. Halfway through the voyage, 110 of 278 sailors on the three no-lemon-juice ships had died of scurvy, while those on the flagship stayed healthy.

Incredibly, Lancaster's experiment was ignored for nearly 150 years! It wasn't until a shipboard physician who knew of Lancaster's findings tried a similar experiment in 1747 that citrus was again evaluated as a cure for scurvy. Eventually, limes became a standard provision in British ships—but not until 1795—another 48 years after Lancaster's results had been confirmed!

The saga of Direct Instruction (DI) is remarkably similar to the story of Lancaster's cure for scurvy. Invented nearly 50 years ago, DI is a scripted, step-by-step approach to teaching that is among the most thoroughly tested and proven in the history of education. It works equally well for general education, gifted students, and the disabled, but surprisingly remains little used.

DI was the clear winner in the federal government's 10-year Follow Through project—the largest study in history to compare different approaches to instruction. In the 40 years since Follow Through, DI has repeatedly been shown to be effective with all kinds of students—from at-risk and struggling preschoolers to top performers in middle school. Yet, despite its demonstrated effectiveness and an acute need for improved schooling outcomes—over two-thirds of all fourth graders are not proficient in reading—most teachers know little about it.

Students love Direct Instruction. They become engaged and excited, not passive and bored. Teachers who become proficient in DI prefer it because of the great results they get with students. Just an hour of DI instruction per day is typically enough to significantly improve student performance.

DI works so well that its author— Siegfried "Zig" Engelmann —has a standing offer to wager $100,000 on a contest between DI and any other type of reading instruction. In forty years, no one has accepted his challenge.

Why isn't DI more popular?

So why isn't DI more popular? Critics—most of them outside the classroom—have a litany of complaints, all duly noted and refuted in this report. Their overriding reservation, however, is that DI contradicts much of what educators are taught to believe about "good" teaching.

DI is old-school. It uses teaching practices that were scorned by Progressive Era reformers but widely used until education was swept up in the cultural revolution of the sixties and seventies. These include teacher-led exercises, skill grouping, choral responding, and repetition. DI also provides a carefully designed and tested script, not just a content outline or lesson plan from which the teacher endeavors to create an effective lesson.

> Students love Direct Instruction. They become engaged and excited, not passive and bored. Teachers who become proficient in DI prefer it because of the great results they get with students. Just an hour of DI instruction per day is typically enough to significantly improve student performance.

Essentially, DI teaches academic lessons the same way great trainers and coaches teach the fundamentals in sports. It identifies key skills, teaches them first, and then adds to that foundation. It builds mastery through practice and intervenes early to prevent bad habits. Unlike virtually any other approach to instruction, it is built on the premise that the program is responsible for the results. If the student has not learned, the program has not taught.

While these features are what make DI so extraordinarily effective, they are

2

profoundly at odds with the beliefs about good teaching that have come to dominate education . DI is rejected not because it doesn't work—it does—but because it challenges the validity of those beliefs.

For decades and especially since the sixties, teachers have been taught to be "a guide on the side, not a sage on the stage." This ideal regards Direct Instruction and similar approaches as the antithesis of good teaching. Thus, education professors and theorists denigrate DI's teacher-led practice as "drill and kill," its high expectations as "developmentally inappropriate," and its emphasis on building a solid foundation of skills as "rote-learning." They complain that DI interferes with teacher autonomy and student creativity, and is otherwise at odds with "best practices."

DI does in fact confine students and teachers to a specific sequence of learning interactions, but by doing so it produces superior results. As studies have repeatedly shown, DI's step-by-step approach is more effective than either the individualized interventions created by teachers or the improvised programs and practices favored by DI's critics. Indeed DI programs are so carefully constructed that some subjects can be taught by a computer. For example in Georgia, high school students using a computer-based version of DI called *Funnix* were more successful in teaching reading to Head Start children than were the regular teaching staff who used conventional methods.

> The training typically received by teachers is not merely flawed, it is detrimental to the aims of standards-based educational reform. Rather than preparing teachers to be confident directors and managers of classroom learning, most teacher preparation programs instill a reluctance to use DI and similar results-oriented methodologies.

The ideal of the teacher as a facilitator of student-led learning activity has hindered the adoption not just of DI but of virtually all teaching practices that are designed to attain specific curricular objectives. In this regard, the training typically received by teachers is not merely flawed, it is detrimental to the aims of standards-based educational reform. Rather than preparing teachers to be confident directors and managers of classroom learning, most teacher preparation programs instill a reluctance to use DI and similar results-oriented methodologies.

Clearly, there are occasions when teachers can be effective as guides and facilitators, but these tend to be in the latter, not the beginning, stages of learning. Beginners progress most quickly and easily when they have clear direction, close monitoring, and encouragement.

School districts can re-train teachers to become classroom leaders and to use methodologies like DI, but doing so is often an uphill battle. To maintain a staff that is capable of carrying out such a program, a district must have leadership, training, and supervision that are capable of making progress against a headwind of collegial skepticism. For that reason, DI programs often sprout but later wither if the charismatic leader who nurtured the program moves on in his or her career.

America's Needs and the Promise of DI

Fortunately, the last 15 years have seen a gradual shift away from theory-driven practices such as whole language reading instruction and toward empirically validated methodologies like Direct Instruction. Extensive assessments of reading instruction by the National Research Council and the National Reading Panel have vindicated the key components of Engelmann's approach while finding many of the popular alternatives to be unproven or invalid.

Direct Instruction is not a silver bullet that can overcome all of America's student achievement challenges, but it can dramatically improve achievement outcomes in key areas like reading and math. Improvement is desperately needed. Not only are two thirds of fourth graders below proficient in reading, 60% are below proficient in math. These are deficiencies that handicap children for the rest of their educational careers, and indeed, the rest of their lives.

> DI confronts what may be America's greatest educational challenge: the enormous numbers of children who are promoted from grade to grade with woefully deficient basic skills.

As learners become discouraged, progress requires increasingly heroic remediation—a significant burden on teachers and an increasing drag on the progress of all students. DI can relieve both of these restrictions on school performance—especially at the middle school level—by greatly reducing the gap between the undertaught high achievers and the overwhelmed low performers.

Teachers and principals who want to know more about Direct Instruction will find Shepard Barbash's *Clear Teaching* to be a worthy introduction. He summarizes the case for DI, supports it with endnotes and appendices, and explains why DI remains controversial among educators despite its record of effectiveness.

More resources on DI are available at **www.ClearTeaching.org**. These include references to video and other online resources as well as contact information for experts, trainers, and speakers who can provide online or onsite introductions to DI.

We ask educators to set aside their theories and preconceptions about learning and to consider the testimonials of formerly skeptical educators who have experienced DI's effectiveness first-hand. DI confronts what may be America's greatest educational challenge: the enormous numbers of children who are promoted from grade to grade with woefully deficient basic skills. The comfort that derives from familiar habits is important, but the children are the top priority.

> After searching for practical and proven options that could have a substantial impact on student achievement, we simply concluded that the use of Direct Instruction in preK-3 would be the single most cost-effective step that most school districts could take.

The Education Consumers Foundation is a consumer organization—like the publisher of Consumer Reports—except that we focus exclusively on education. We are an independent non-profit and have no financial connection to or interest in Direct Instruction or any other education program. After searching for practical and proven options that could have a substantial impact on student achievement, we simply concluded that the use of Direct Instruction in preK-3 would be the single most cost-effective step that most school districts could take.

We at ECF believe that the educational failures in America's public schools are not the inevitable product of a child's social and economic circumstances; rather, they reflect a man-made dilemma that can be substantially alleviated by more effective schooling—especially by better preK-3 reading instruction. Success in early schooling will not guarantee future school success, but it will greatly enhance the chances of success for the approximately 70% of America's children who now face very long odds. Until something more dependable and cost-effective is demonstrated, we believe that Direct Instruction is the best way to improve those odds for millions of children.

J. E. Stone, Ed.D.
President
Education Consumers Foundation
www.education-consumers.org

CLEAR TEACHING

INTRODUCTION

What if Charles Darwin had written *The Origin of Species* and nobody noticed? Or Copernicus had shown that the earth went around the sun and nobody believed him? Or Jonas Salk had found a cure for polio and nobody cared? Such has been the fate of Siegfried Engelmann, pioneering inventor of a better way to teach that almost nobody uses.

Engelmann has spent the last 50 years working out answers to basic questions every good teacher asks. What should I teach my students? How can I teach them so that they *all* learn what I'm trying to teach? How can I accelerate their learning as much as possible and help those who are behind? How do I know in what order to teach things and what not to teach at all? How will I know *right away* if a student is learning or is confused and needs help? *How* do I re-teach? How do I get my students to pay attention and work hard? How do I get them to trust me? How do I get them to trust themselves? In sum, how can I become the best teacher possible?

Unlike education theorists whose vague ideas rarely help anyone in the class-room, Engelmann stands alone for his ability to design clear instructional programs that can accelerate learning in even the hardest to teach children and that any willing teacher can learn to use. Known as Direct Instruction, his approach puts teachers firmly in charge of their students' learning and gives them a reliable, cost-effective way to verify how well they are actually teaching.

More scientific evidence validates the effectiveness of his methods than any other approach to instruction.

Engelmann has written more than a hundred curricula using Direct Instruction (DI) principles, covering all the major subjects from preschool to high school. He tests his programs in the classroom, and uses the results to improve them. He has taught every program he has designed and has trained others meticulously in his methods. More scientific evidence validates the effectiveness of his methods than any other approach to instruction. Yet so different are his techniques and curricula from anything else in education that even now, after so many years, few educators understand them, few colleges teach them, and barely 2% of K-12 teachers use them. Like Copernicus, whose proofs were rejected by the Church for 300 years, Engelmann remains a scorned revolutionary, anathema or simply unknown to most people in his field.

CHAPTER I:
RADICAL OPTIMIST

"If the student hasn't learned, the teacher hasn't taught."

There is no quick or easy way to summarize Engelmann's approach to teaching. A concise description of his principles, *Rubric for Identifying Authentic Direct Instruction Programs*, runs 109 pages. But his main idea is as clear and as radical as the Declaration of Independence: Engelmann believes that the mind of every child, even the least impressive, is an incredible thinking machine gifted with extraordinary powers to learn.

"We begin with the obvious fact that the children we work with are perfectly capable of learning anything that we have to teach," he declares in *Theory of Instruction*, the book that most fully describes his ideas and methods and the evidence supporting them. "We know that the intellectual crippling of children is caused overwhelmingly by faulty instruction—not by faulty children."

How radical is Engelmann's optimism about kids and his willingness to take responsibility for their failures? The best evidence comes from a study that reviewed the cases of 5,000 students who were evaluated by school psychologists to determine why they were doing poorly in class. All 5,000 evaluations attributed the student's problems to deficiencies *in the child* and the child's family. *Not one* linked the student's problems to faulty curricula, poor teaching practices or bad school management. (The study's findings were published by Galen Alessi in 1988 and replicated by Barrie Wade and Maggie Moore five years later.)

> "We know that the intellectual crippling of children is caused overwhelmingly by faulty instruction—not by faulty children."

Such bias is the bitter fruit of learning theories that fail to see how—and how much—a child's mind is shaped by exactly what the teacher communicates to it. "It's not the teacher's fault, it's the theorists' fault," Engelmann says. "They're the ones who are backwards." *Constructivists* say the mind creates its own knowledge largely through its own efforts. *Learning styles* theorists say different minds learn the same things in physiologically different ways, requiring different teaching methods for different children. *Developmentalists* say the mind matures in phases we cannot change—a notion derived from the theories of Swiss psychologist Jean Piaget, who believed that a child's mental abilities developed in age-determined phases. Hence if a child fails to learn something, it's not because the teaching is faulty; it's because the child is either *developmentally disabled* or not yet *developmentally ready* to learn it. These theories may sound reasonable—as geocentrism did before Copernicus—but they have not held up when tested in the classroom. They in fact misapprehend the intricacies of how we learn and the power of teaching to accelerate the process.

Engelmann's theory is that a child's mind is entirely logical in the way it learns, and that what or how much it learns depends on how logically it is taught. "The learning process is the same for all learners," he says. The mind does not construct its own private knowledge of fractions, or sentences, or the qualities of a chocolate bar, without data about the details of these concepts. Computation, comprehension, and candy all possess their own unchanging features, which must somehow be taught to learners of diverse abilities and starting points. What the mind *does* construct, Engelmann says, is a rule—a rule that the mind derives from what the teacher conveys to it. If the teacher's presentation generates only one rule or meaning, all minds that have the necessary background knowledge will learn that meaning, *regardless of their other differences*. If the presentation implies more than one meaning, all minds will still learn *something* logical from what's presented. The problem is, they may not all learn the same thing, and what they learn may be wrong and not what we want them to learn. Engelmann calls these mistakes *misrules*, and says the key to avoiding

> A study reviewed the cases of 5,000 students who were evaluated by school psychologists to determine why they were doing poorly in class. All 5,000 evaluations attributed the student's problems to deficiencies *in the child* and the child's family. Not one linked the student's problems to faulty curricula, poor teaching practices, or bad school management.

them is to control the teacher's input. Learning failures thus derive not from some illogic or idiosyncrasy or immaturity of the child's mind—as the reigning theories assert—but from technical problems the teacher can readily correct: ambiguous communication, the learner's lack of necessary background knowledge, or inadequate practice to master what is presented. Fix these problems and the mind will learn. It is wired to do so.

Engelmann did not formulate these principles from books or from abstract speculation about the way children learn. He formulated them through a painstaking process of trial and error in the classroom, then applied them to create a series of unique programs that outperform others in their power to teach many different subjects, to all kinds of children. His ideas have shown great predictive power: of the 55 studies conducted to test the validity of different assertions in *Theory of Instruction*, 54 confirmed the hypothesis tested. The largest scientific experiment ever to compare different approaches to instruction in the early grades, sponsored by the federal government in the 1970s and known as Project Follow Through, examined 22 methods of instruction and found only one that accelerated the academic achievement of poor children. That winning method was Engelmann's Direct Instruction. *(See chart on next page.)*

Engelmann did not formulate these principles from books or from abstract speculation about the way children learn. He formulated them through a painstaking process of trial and error in the classroom.

Engelmann's theory also predicts what *won't* work. Not only can Engelmann correctly diagnose the types of problems different programs are likely to cause the teachers and students who go through them—he can often tell which programs teachers are using simply by observing the mistakes their students make. He does this not by speculating on the inner workings of the student's mind but by analyzing hard data: the procedures and examples the program uses and whether they are logically capable of generating inappropriate inferences and confusion.

Project Follow Through, 1967 - 1977

Nine models of teaching K-3 compared in history's largest educational experiment

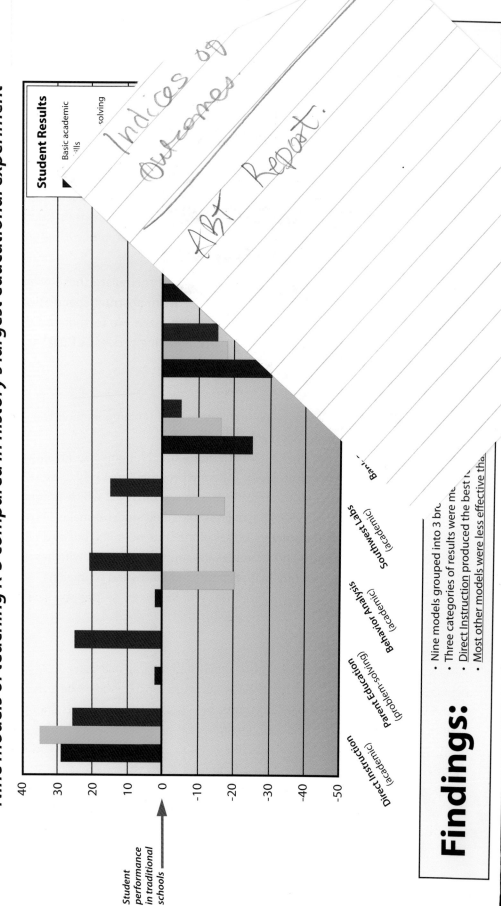

Student Results

- Basic academic skills
- solving

Student performance in traditional schools

Direct Instruction (academic)
Parent Education (problem-solving)
Behavior Analysis (academic)
Southwest Labs (academic)

(handwritten note) Indices of Outcomes — ABT Report.

Findings:

- Nine models grouped into 3 br...
- Three categories of results were m...
- Direct Instruction produced the best r...
- Most other models were less effective tha...

CHAPTER II:
ENGELMANN'S ODYSSEY

From Advertising to Education

Engelmann came to education after many twists and turns. Raised on the south side of Chicago, the son of a doctor and a nurse, he loafed through high school without reading a book, dropped out of college, worked on oil rigs, in a steel mill and at a warehouse (the night shift), went back to school, graduated with honors in philosophy, married and had kids, sold cars, edited a children's encyclopedia (the science section), sold his services as an investment advisor, then went into advertising.

His turning point was an odd one. The pennywise president of a candy company wanted to know how many times kids would need to be exposed to a sales pitch for a chocolate bar before they remembered it well enough to go buy the product. Engelmann surveyed the research on learning and memory and found to his surprise that it was mute on the question. A fiercely inquisitive problem solver, he set up a class to see what it took to teach kids different slogans and became enthralled by the bigger question—how can we help the mind learn? He began teaching his twin sons, got good at it, and made a 30-minute film of them solving linear equations as four-year-olds. Confident he'd be able to find work writing educational programs, he quit his advertising job, shopped his film to 26 different publishers, and was ignored or rejected by them all. He was finally hired as a research associate by the Institute for Research on Exceptional Children at the University of Illinois at Champaign-Urbana. It was 1964.

> The Bereiter-Engelmann preschool was the first to show that the academic achievement gap between rich and poor could be closed, and that early intervention with an hour or two of well-designed instruction per day was the key to closing it.

Direct Instruction grew out of an experiment Engelmann performed that summer to see what young children could learn when taught with the same techniques he had developed teaching his sons. His goal was to show that *all* children, not just precocious ones, could learn much more and much faster than any theorist predicted. He took two groups of three- to five-year-olds—one white and affluent, one black and poor—and within a few weeks taught them things Piaget said couldn't be taught before age 11 or 12: sophisticated concepts like relative direction (A is north of B but south of C), conservation of substance, and the behavior of light entering and leaving a mirror. Having done the 'impossible,' he was nevertheless disappointed. He had predicted that if the teaching were designed carefully enough, both groups would learn new material at the same rate, but to his consternation, the rich kids learned faster. He traced the difference to a severe language deficit in the African-American group—now commonly called the language gap—and resolved to figure out how to overcome it. Within a month he and his colleagues Carl Bereiter and Jean Osborn had opened the most revolutionary preschool in America.

The Bereiter-Engelmann preschool, as it came to be called, was the first to show that the academic achievement gap between rich and poor could be closed, and that early intervention with an hour or two of well-designed instruction per day was the key to closing it. Open half-days and serving poor families, the preschool resembled others in that children were encouraged to play, sing songs, listen to stories and get along with each other. What made it unique was that for twenty to thirty minutes two or three times a day, they were taught skills in language, read-

ing and math whose mastery Engelmann understood to be critical to their future academic success.

The school dramatically accelerated learning even in the most verbally deprived four-year-olds. Children who entered the preschool unable to count to ten and not knowing the meaning of "under," "over," or "Stand up!" went into kindergarten reading and doing math at a second-grade level. Confounding the belief that intelligence was hereditary, Engelmann found (and others later confirmed) that the mean IQ for the group jumped from 96 to 121 in one year—the largest IQ gains ever recorded in a group of children. He also found that, contrary to popular belief, kids *enjoyed* learning hard things from adults, and gained confidence as they gained skills. Most important, he found that the results did not depend on him or a few gifted colleagues: he could write programs that allowed most people to use his methods after some training. Teachers using early versions of Engelmann's *Language for Learning*, *Reading Mastery*, and *Connecting Math Concepts* achieved results well above the norm for poor children in nine preschools and more than thirty elementary schools across the country in the 1970s.

But Engelmann also found that while parents encouraged their schools to adopt DI, colleges of education opposed and attacked it. The University of Illinois in particular would not let him train student teachers. He approached every teacher training program he could find that had a stated mission to help the poor. Only two showed any interest. His first choice was Temple University in Philadelphia, but Temple backed out after two faculty departments voted unanimously against his appointment. He then accepted a position in the College of Education at the University of Oregon, thousands of miles from most of the schools where he was then working. He moved to Eugene in 1970, and retired from the university in 2003.

CHAPTER III:
ENGELMANN DID IT FIRST

A Pioneering Scientist in the Field of Education

To paraphrase a best-seller, all we really need to know about instruction Engelmann learned teaching preschool. His list of discoveries and inventions rivals that of any great scientist.

He was the first to figure out that to learn to read one must first be able to hear *and* manipulate the sounds that make up words—a skill others recognized only decades later and gave a fancy name: *phonemic awareness* (a phoneme is a unit of sound). He was the first to appreciate the significance of the language gap between middle-class and poor students (a gap quantified by researchers Betty Hart and Todd Risley 30 years later) and to create programs that enabled teachers to close it. He is one of the unrecognized pioneers of modern cognitive psychology—the study of how the mind thinks, learns and remembers.

Scholarly literature today is filled with findings that explain and justify what Engelmann put into his programs forty years earlier. *Developmental Psychology*, for instance, recently reported the results of a study showing that the ability to understand and follow directions predicts the ability to learn math. Engelmann's very first program, *Language for Learning*, written to bridge the language gap, teaches children to pay close attention to the teacher by giving them tricky commands like "When the teacher says 'Go!'—stand up" or "If the teacher says 'Now!'—hold up your hand." Children also learn to follow sequences of directions like: "Take your coat off, hang it up, sit down, and take out your book." Engelmann's first math programs anticipated research showing the sequence by which young children develop number sense: the ability to count, compare number values, recognize patterns, and understand what number symbols stand for. His reading programs anticipated the discovery that comprehension depends on background knowledge, general language

> **Scholarly literature today is filled with findings that explain and justify what Engelmann put into his programs forty years earlier.**

skill (not simply vocabulary), and the ability to decode words fluently. They also anticipated findings on the amount of practice needed to learn and remember new words. Engelmann was also ahead of the research showing that students are more motivated to work hard when they are set up to succeed and when they can see that they are making progress on meaningful tasks.

Response to Intervention, now touted as a major advance in how children are diagnosed and taught for special education, reinvents another Engelmann wheel. RTI requires screening and placement of students based on a careful assessment of their abilities, frequent assessments to monitor their progress, and scientifically validated instruction adjusted frequently to meet the student's evolving needs. The Bereiter-Engelmann preschool did much the same thing, with greater scientific rigor and without labeling any child *disabled*.

Another new tool, magnetic resonance imaging (MRI), vindicates Engelmann's abiding faith that the human mind is malleable and magnificent. MRIs have shown that scientifically-based instruction like DI produces lasting and beneficial changes in the brain, thereby confirming in the lab what Engelmann through logical analysis and experience in the classroom found to be true: every child has a wondrous capacity to learn, every teacher has a unique opportunity to help.

CHAPTER IV:
RULES, NOT MISRULES

"What humans learn is perfectly consistent with the input they receive."

Making up rules to make sense of things is an involuntary operation that goes on continuously in all of us. It defines our thinking humanity and gives teachers enormous power to shape a child's mind: to lead it to clarity or confusion with words, actions and models. Indeed Piaget and others who paint pictures of the child's lockstep mental development get it wrong. Engelmann shows that learning is in fact a highly choreograph-able dance between the mind and its surroundings, not an unchanging, self-directed march inside the brain. And in class the teacher leads the dance.

"Teaching is a manipulative science or art," he writes in *Conceptual Learning*. "The teacher changes the learner only through the manipulation of environmental variables." Doing it right is not easy. To make sure a child learns the right rule, and especially to avoid learning wrong rules (what Engelmann calls *misrules*), Direct Instruction demands the precision of aircraft design in its programs and the responsiveness of a jazz musician in its delivery.

DI's beating heart is curriculum—curriculum designed by Engelmann and as unique to him as a Bach fugue is to Bach. One way to explain how his programs work is to use his own teaching methods to explain them. One of Engelmann's most important strategies is to find a rule or idea that can be used to explain the biggest chunk of content possible, thereby organizing the subject matter for the teacher and reducing the memory load on the student. Thus in earth science, one rule might be: when something gets hot it expands. (This principle helps explain everything from the formation of continents, seas and mountains to the vagaries of weather.) Direct Instruction boils down to five big rules.

Rule Number 1: Be Clear

Try this experiment. Make up a nonsense word for a familiar concept and try teaching the concept to someone without using its regular name.

Engelmann holds up a pencil and says, "This is *glerm*." Then he holds up a pen and says, "This is *glerm*." Then he holds up a crayon—also *glerm*. So what is *glerm*? A student responds: "Something you write with." Logical, but wrong, Engelmann says. *Glerm* means *up*. The student learned a misrule—Engelmann's examples were deliberately ambiguous, exempli-fying both the concepts for *up* and for writing implements, and the student came to the wrong con-clusion. This is one of the exercises Engelmann uses to teach instruc-tional design. His point is to make us aware of the minefield teachers must navigate to avoid generating confusion in their students.

The reading teacher runs an obstacle course of potential misrules. Teach with a picture book and some children will infer that words are deciphered by looking at pictures. Teach with a rhyming book and some will infer that words can always be deciphered by looking at their first letter.

Next he wanders around the room giving examples of the concept *graeb*, with-out success. At last he opens the door, walks out and shouts: "This is not *graeb*." *Graeb* means *in the room*. To show what something *is*, sometimes you have to show what it's *not*. He points to a cup on his desk and says, "That's *glick*." Then he holds up a spoon and says, "Not *glick*." He points to a book on a student's desk—*glick*—then raises a pen—*not glick*. What's *glick*? No one is sure. Finally he puts the spoon on his desk—that's *glick*—lifts it—not *glick*—puts the pen on the student's desk—*glick*—and lifts it—not *glick*. Everyone gets it: *glick* means *on*.

19

"The mind is lawful," Engelmann says. "What humans learn is perfectly consistent with the input they receive. The simplest object you can find, like a piece of paper, is an example of an indefinitely large number of concepts. It follows that if you want to teach one of the things for which paper is an example"—a rectangle, or something to write on, or something white or thin or lightweight or useable to make spitballs or toy airplanes—"you have to order your presentation of examples so that you rule out all the other possibilities. That can be hard to do. But if there is more than one possible interpretation of what you've presented, some of your kids are going to pick up on the wrong one. The lower performing your kids are, the more often they'll pick up on unintended interpretations."

Perhaps the most common and debilitating misrule concerns fractions. Most adults when asked will say a fraction is a number less than one. That's because as children we were introduced to the concept with a misleading set of examples—one-half, one-third, one-fourth. "The biggest problem teaching higher math to kids is they don't understand fractions, so they can't manipulate them," Engelmann says. "After spending months working on problems where the numerator is always one, they are unable to generalize to problems like *two-thirds of nine* or *four-thirds of twelve*. They don't understand what the numbers mean." *(See sidebar, What is Blue?)*

The reading teacher runs an obstacle course of potential misrules. Teach with a picture book and some children will infer that words are deciphered by looking at pictures. Teach with a rhyming book and some will infer that words can always be deciphered by looking at their first letter. Tell them to figure out a strange

What is Blue?

Engelmann on Teaching Clearly

Engelmann's methods emphasize learning rules, but they put almost as much emphasis on not learning (or not *teaching*) misrules. Once a child constructs a misrule in class, it takes a great deal of effort to fix it—and even years later, the misrule can come back in many guises to obstruct future progress.

"Whatever concept you're teaching," Engelmann says, "the rule is to present the full range of examples for it as soon as possible, and to choose examples that will lead the student to generate rules and infer things about the concept that will not be contradicted later on. If you're teaching *blue*, you wouldn't just show four blue toasters or four blue cars or a fleet of cars a hundred shades of blue. You'd have a blue car, a blue bird, a blue sky, a blue lake, maybe a blue table. You'd show that whether or not something is *blue* has nothing to do with whether it's solid, liquid, touchable, not touchable, living or not living. Then you'd teach *not blue* by showing examples that were the same *except* for their color. And you'd choose colors that were close to blue. You might show three identical birds, one blue, one purple and one green. You'd point to the blue one and say *blue* and point to the other two birds and say *not blue*.

"If you're teaching fractions, you give them examples to work with early on that show that fractions are not always less than one and do not always have a numerator of one. You tell them the bottom number tells how many parts are in each group, and the top number tells how many parts you use. You make sure they understand that the bottom number, if it's 4, doesn't tell you to make only one group with 4 in it, it tells you that however many groups you have, each group has 4 parts. The top number tells you how many of those parts you're going to use. If the top number is 3, you color 3 parts; if it's 7 you color 7 parts, which means of course that you're going to have more than one whole group. It's very easy then to teach kids fractions that are more than one and less than one. You teach the mainline stuff first: any combination of positive numbers that the kids already know. Once you're solid on those, everything else is going to be a minor variation—negative numbers, letters in fractions, fractions over fractions. *But here's the test. Can you teach all this stuff without ever contradicting anything you taught earlier?* If you can, you have a good system, with great acceleration potential down the pike. If you start implying something different or suggesting new inferences, then you've done it wrong. *You should never have to change your basic view about what fractions are from the first day you learn about them.*"

word by looking at how long it is, or by thinking of words that make sense in the context, and some will infer that the length of a word or its placement with others tells more about the word than the letters in the word itself. Teach new letters by presenting them always at the beginning of words, and some kids will have problems identifying the letter when it appears in the *middle* of a word. Teach letters by turning them into familiar objects—an *h* made to look like a house, for instance—and some will confuse houses with *h's* and will be unable to recognize normal *h's* in regular fonts. Teach *sounding out* for too long and some kids will become confused by words like *said* and *was* because they can't be sounded out.

> DI programs are designed to teach more in less time and at *less cost*. The goal is to accelerate learning in all children, but particularly in low performers who are behind their peers.

Every subject is fraught with possible misrules. DI programs help teachers cope with this dilemma by specifying the precise sequence of examples, tasks and wording they need to teach their subjects clearly.

DI programs are also clear about what students should be able to do by the end of the program. Students who complete *Essentials for Algebra*, for instance, should have mastered the topics that appear on the high school exit exams of most states. Students who complete *Spelling Through Morphographs* should be able to spell most of the 27,000 most frequently used words in English.

Rule Number Two: Be Efficient

DI programs are designed to teach more in less time and at *less cost*. The goal is to accelerate learning in all children, but particularly in low performers who are behind their peers.

Engelmann's strategies to achieve efficiency are what make DI look so different from other programs. The most important and most difficult is to figure out what to teach when—and, as noted, to uncover the broadest common features of the subject so that students can be taught broadly applicable rules and procedures. Rather than approach knowledge as an encyclopedia to be mastered, DI programs take advantage of the mind's instinct to generalize by teaching it algorithms (series of steps) that enable it to solve many problems, and conceptual frameworks that enable it to learn, organize and remember many facts.

Consider the task of teaching letters and the sounds they make. English has 26 letters, at least 44 sounds, and at least 220 spelling patterns to indicate those sounds. Children are expected to memorize all of them as they learn to read. Engelmann in his programs uses several strategies to teach them faster. In *Reading Mastery*, he teaches the sounds first before the letter names so that children are able to get into reading faster. In *Horizons*, designed for higher performers, he teaches letter names but shows how the names for most consonants are related to the sounds the letters make in words. For the letters *f l m n r s* and *x*, the *last* part of the letter name is the sound it makes (e.g., the name *e-SSS*, and *e-LLL*). For the letters *b d j k p v z* and *t*, the *first* part of the letter name is the sound it makes (e.g., *Teeee*). The programs teach only the 60 most commonly used sound-symbol relationships. (For instance, students are taught the sound *ch* makes in chicken but not in Michigan.) The less common cases can be taught much faster later on, after students have mastered the sounding-out game.

Efficiency is even more important when teaching language, a much vaster domain. Many at-risk children come to school not knowing enough words to understand simple directions such as "Get in a straight line" or "Take out your blue crayon." In their book, *Meaningful Differences in the Everyday Experience of Young American Children*, Hart and Risley found that by the age of three, children from families headed by parents who were professionals had heard, on average, more than three times as many words as children from welfare families—more than 8 million more words. The professional-family kids themselves had spoken more than 4 million more words than the welfare children. The oral vocabularies of the professional-family kids exceeded those not just of the children but of the *parents* of the welfare families. This astonishing language gap correlates closely with large and lifelong deficits in vocabulary and reading ability.

Smart choices about what to teach at-risk kids are essential. "You can't reproduce the *form* of the middle-class upbringing, you've got to try to reproduce the *function*," Engelmann says. "What do at-risk kid most need to know?—the language of instruction. Teaching vocabulary will get you hundreds of words when you need hundreds of thousands. You need to focus on those broad concepts that will permit the kid to develop the skills necessary to follow whatever directions the teacher gives him." DI programs like *Language for Learning* and *Language for Thinking* teach children how to ask and answer questions in complete sentences, sort objects into classes, identify opposites and similarities, use prepositions, synonyms and if/then statements, create definitions for objects, and recognize logical absurdities. Students also learn basic fact systems: numbers, the calendar, and classes of things such as animals, vehicles, colors and tools. *(See the Appendix, "Reinforcing Success: Snapshot of a DI Class")*

The most visible efficiency features of DI programs are concise teacher scripts and choral student responses. The scripts eliminate extraneous teacher talk, which often unintentionally confuses students. The choral response maximizes the number of times individual children respond, per minute, per period. The script makes it possible for the experienced teacher to present 9-12 tasks per minute. If there are twenty children in the group and all respond to each task, the teacher teaches far more children per minute than would be possible by calling on them one at a time. The choral responses provide feedback on the children's understanding. (A teacher trained in Engelmann's methods will hear when students answer late or incorrectly—just as an orchestra conductor hears a violinist who comes in late or off-key.) Both features maximize oral practice for the student and timely feedback to the teacher.

One of the most powerful efficiency tools unique to Engelmann is the *hot verbal sequence*—a carefully sequenced chain of examples that the teacher presents and students respond to in unison at a very high rate. The speed is essential to cement students' learning because the memory decays rapidly on new and unfamiliar material. A typical hot verbal series generates as many as 15 exchanges per minute. Indeed the most famous line Engelmann ever wrote is probably "Next word, what word?"—a model of brevity and clarity that DI reading teachers say a hundred or more times a day to give students practice with new words. (Engelmann had tried the phrase, "What is the next word?" and found it slower and harder for teachers to say.)

> DI classes comprise children who perform at about the same level. The combination of ability grouping and unison response brings the instruction as close to one-on-one as possible in a group setting, allowing teachers to differentiate instruction more efficiently.

One of the *least* visible means by which DI teaches more in less time is to gauge precisely where a student should be placed in a program. Students are properly placed at the point where they perform correctly at least 70% of the time when introduced to new material. Anything below that rate and the student will struggle too much. Ideally, DI classes comprise children who perform at about the same level. The combination of ability grouping and unison response brings the instruction as close to one-on-one as possible in a group setting, allowing teachers to differentiate instruction more efficiently.

Of course the best way to be efficient is to avoid confusing your students. Relearning something that has been learned incorrectly takes three to seven times longer than learning it correctly the first time. Many programs cause confusion by introducing similar concepts together: numerator/denominator, quart/gallon, week/month, hour hand/minute hand. DI programs separate them. The student masters one, and so is less likely to get confused encountering the other. (Just as if we meet two guys at a party named Hansel and Hanson, we are more likely to confuse them than we would if we had already known one of them for a while.)

Letters are easily confused. They are the first things children encounter whose identity depends on their orientation. Turn a chair back and forth, flip it upside down, turn it back and forth again—it's still a chair. Not so with letters. What the child assumes from experience will be the same object suddenly becomes a *b* or a *d* or a *q* or a *p* depending on its orientation. Engelmann's core reading program, *Reading Mastery*, teaches *b* and *d* 20 lessons apart.

Rule Number Three: Teach to Mastery

Speed must not come at the expense of thoroughness. DI programs are designed to teach things so thoroughly that a student never forgets them. Engelmann manages this in two steps. First, he identifies in detail all the skills that go into performing a task and arranges them into a logical sequence for teaching. Then, he lays out the instruction to make sure students get enough practice to master each new concept or skill.

Differences in *learning rates* for students in effective programs tend to be smaller than differences in *starting points*—what students start out knowing how to do—but the former are exacerbated when we fail to acknowledge and address the latter. "The most important rule, and possibly the most difficult one to teach teachers, is that you have to start as close as possible to where the learner performs, and you have to teach to mastery," Engelmann says. "You can't achieve mastery if you introduce tasks that are far beyond the learner's ability, and if you don't give kids enough practice."

> Differences in *learning rates* for students in effective programs tend to be smaller than differences in *starting points*—what students start out knowing how to do—but the former are exacerbated when we fail to acknowledge and address the latter.

Repetition is the mother of memory, a Latin proverb says. At-risk students rarely are given enough practice to master the skills they need. That's because most of us forget how much time and effort it takes to learn and remember new things. Once we master something we feel like we've always known it. Indeed, we can't imagine *not* knowing it. Even as we learn it, we are unaware of the knowledge and habits of mind we may have that help us learn it.

Some beginning readers will need a lot more practice than others to master the alphabetic code or remember the meaning of a new word. How much practice in either case depends in part on what the learner already knows going into the task. Children with parents who talk to them a lot will have learned more than their less fortunate peers about sounds, words and the learning process itself, so they will learn to read faster. The same holds true for memorizing math facts, scientific concepts, or musical notes. "Fast learners" are fast in part because they have less to learn.

Engelmann is meticulous about designing programs that teach to mastery. Each DI curriculum is a staircase, each lesson a step. Each step comprises at most 15% new material and 85% reinforcement of things already taught. The effect is to impart "a systematic trickle of new information" that accelerates learning but at no point inundates the learner with too much too fast. Content is arranged in strands that extend across several lessons; each lesson extends several strands. Everything learned is applied over and over and in different contexts. Seemingly isolated skills are taught and combined with other skills to teach more complex skills. Some DI programs take six weeks to complete and some take six years, but all are designed to make learning as error-free and free of gaps as possible. Engelmann creates placement tests so sensitive they tell teachers not only which grade level but which *lesson* the learner should start in a program (i.e., the one in which the learner can do at least 70% of the tasks correctly on the first try). He also creates mastery tests after every five to ten lessons so that teachers can make informed and timely decisions about what to do next—whether to go on to the next lesson, re-teach students A and B some things, or jump student C ahead in the program. He field-tests programs prior to publication to see how much and what kind of practice students need to

> Repetition is the mother of memory, a Latin proverb says. At-risk students rarely are given enough practice to master the skills they need. That's because most of us forget how much time and effort it takes to learn and remember new things.

26

master specific concepts and relationships, and he revises the programs as needed to make sure they get it.

Practice makes permanent; perfect practice makes perfect. *How* students get their practice matters as much as *how much* practice they get. Engelmann pioneered the Model—Lead—Test technique: demonstrate a task, do it with the students, observe them as they do it alone. If they make a mistake, correct immediately and succinctly. (Delayed feedback doesn't work very well because students forget.)

Correcting is in fact the hardest skill for teachers to master, but it's among the most important. "A correction procedure that makes sense to the learner is the coin of the realm," Engelmann says. DI programs help teachers with corrections in three ways: Content is carefully arranged so that when a student errs, the mistake can be corrected by re-teaching something taught earlier in the program. Tasks are explicit and specific enough to be correctable. And different correction procedures, though they obviously can't be scripted, are specified for a range of errors. For instance: never repeat a wrong answer before giving the right one—it reinforces the confusion. When correcting a decodable word, don't say the word—ask the student to try sounding it out again. When correcting a *sound*, say the right sound and have the student repeat it.

> Practice makes permanent; perfect practice makes perfect. *How* students get their practice matters as much as *how much* practice they get.

Student errors should not be seen as problems, but as valuable information, Engelmann says. "They tell you *exactly* what you need to teach at any given moment to bring your students to mastery, so that testing and teaching become the same package."

Rule Number Four: Celebrate Success

There are as many ways for teachers to encourage students as there are teachers and students, but none will work well for long if neither side feels like they're good at what they're doing. DI programs are designed to encourage self-confidence and effort by laying out a rapid series of tasks that teachers can help their students to master, usually on their first try. Both sides get to celebrate success every time a student gets the right answer, which in DI programs is hundreds of times a day. Over and over teachers can take pleasure in saying the words children (like the rest of us) long to hear: Good job! Boy, you're smart! Over and over students can

Kids Beat Teacher
The Fooler Game

Some people try to get inner-city kids to work hard for cash. DI teachers get them to work hard for strips of paper and a handshake.

Even more than money, what most kids want is respect, love, and yes, *victory*. Link any reward to the prospect of obtaining those things and the reward will be effective. One way to do that is to play the fooler game.

Engelmann explains the rules to a kindergarten class. "Let's play the fooler game," he says. "I'm going to touch these letters and say the sounds they make, and if I make a mistake you've got to catch it. If you don't, I get a point; if you do, *you* get a point. But watch out. I'm good at this game, I'm smarter than you, and I'm going to beat ya' real bad." The game is rigged for learning. Students can win, but only by paying close attention. If they miss a sound, they are motivated to get it right the next time because *getting it right* means not just learning the sound but *beating the teacher* and not getting fooled. Engelmann loses the game narrowly and exclaims, "You got lucky today, but I'll get you next time!" "No you won't!" the kids shout.

Rewards are attached to the fooler game, but these need be no more than tokens to get kids playing, and even these can be phased out with time. The token depends on the kid. Some will work for a Fruit Loop. Others will work to get ten minutes extra recess or to make their teacher do a 'happy dance' or give them a 'wet-noodle' handshake. Engelmann, a big man, once brought order to group of rambunctious four-year-olds by flexing his bicep and promising to let them touch it after their lesson if they worked hard. (They worked hard!) On entering the room he lit a match to seize the group's attention and let the littlest kid blow it out.

How a teacher *treats* the reward, more than the reward itself, shapes how kids think of it. "Teaching is like acting," Engelmann says. "A trainee I worked with, Paul, would come back each day totally down. 'I can't get 'em started, I can't control 'em,' he says. So I went in with M&Ms. 'Time to work,' I say. I ask them a question, nobody answers. I ask another. One kid answers. I give him two M&Ms. 'Good job!' After about four questions I had 'em all. If they made a mistake, I ate an M&M. For one task, I took out three M&Ms. 'This is the hardest task of all, you're *never* going to get it,' I say. Of course they all got it. And I acted terribly disappointed that I had to give them three M&Ms and couldn't eat them myself.

"A month later I come back and Paul couldn't buckle his belt. He'd gained 18 pounds eating M&Ms. 'Take 'em off the candy!' I say. 'No way!' he says. 'I remember how they were before.' 'But they're not the same kids now. They're not working for the M&Ms, they're working because they know they're succeeding. They're very proud of what they're doing.' Next day I cut out a pile of strips of yellow paper and went to class. 'What's the most M&Ms you've ever earned for a task?' Three. 'Okay, this next task is worth *four* M&Ms or'—I hold up a piece of yellow paper. 'I know what you're going to choose because you're kids, and like kids you'll choose the M&Ms. Yum! Yum! But *adults* will often work for certificates—symbols that show they're smart—and the symbol sometimes will just be a piece of paper. So here we go.' I present a task. They all answer correctly. 'What do you want?' I ask, and I reach for the M&Ms. Every kid in the group but one picked the yellow paper. But at that point they weren't doing it for the paper. They were doing it for the real reinforcement: the idea that they were doing better than the teacher—that these were all contests, and they were winning, and it was evidence that they were smart and could show the teacher just how smart they were."

feel that the praise they're getting is sincere, well-earned, and true: they *are* doing a good job. They're learning important things. What could be more encouraging?

Of course, it's not so easy. Managing a classroom can be like flying a small airplane through a storm. How can the teacher make students on different learning curves all feel good about themselves while still teaching them all to mastery? How should the teacher respond to behavior and *shape* behavior? What magic words will reach the apathetic, charm the defiant, and calm the fearful? There is no script for these interactions.

"You always have to be thinking," one DI teacher says. "There's a lot of heavy decision-making going on. You don't check your brains at the door."

Engelmann has found that much of what works goes against our instincts. Our natural impulse is to devote more energy to correcting bad behavior than to praising the good. But pay attention to a behavior and it tends to increase, not decrease. (Try telling a small boy to stop bouncing his leg.) The trick is to turn our own behavior upside down and make a concerted effort to 'catch kids being good'—to praise much more than we blame. We should praise pointedly and specifically ("I like how you stopped reading at the period") and stop misbehavior without much ado. This is hard to do in any case, but it is next to impossible when teachers and students are floundering in a curriculum that doesn't work well. DI programs make it easier because they generate such high rates of correct responses. Off-task behavior diminishes because children are kept busy with tasks they can succeed at, and because in the end, what kids really cling to is not the behavior itself—good or bad—but the teacher's attention and affection.

Reinforcement is also tricky. "Most programs try to seduce kids with a big come-on up front," Engelmann says. "That's backwards. You want to put your most reinforcing activity at the *end* of the lesson; otherwise what follows the reinforcing stuff will always be a letdown. The kid thinks, 'Boy, I thought I was going to have all this fun, but look at the crap we're doin' *now!*'" That is why children in DI's early reading programs see pictures with a story only after they have mastered the story.

Many adults think the best way to reinforce children is to smile and be nice. There are in fact better ways. "If you can set the kids up to fool you and make you look bad by accomplishing something you said they couldn't do, *that's* reinforcing to them," Engelmann says. (See "The Fooler Game" sidebar.)

Kids are lawful in what they like just as they are lawful in what they learn. They don't like to do things that are punishing, and many find schoolwork punishing. They don't see the goals as worthwhile, and they don't get meaningful evidence that their effort makes any difference. The teacher must somehow bring them to believe both that their learning matters, and that the teacher cares about their learning. It is an instructional challenge, like teaching reading and math. The trick is to change students' *feelings* about school by changing their *knowledge* about themselves and about their own abilities.

Sincerity counts. Empty encouragement is no encouragement at all. "Kids are not stupid," Engelmann says. "They know when they're failing, and they know when a teacher really cares." The teacher's job is not to become the students' friend but to prove to them that they can *succeed*: that the work they find worthless and hard is in fact easy and worthwhile. That is what DI programs help teachers do.

Rule Number Five: Beware Intuition

Intuition is the student's best friend and the teacher's worst enemy. It makes future learning easier, and it makes it harder for us to teach what we know to others. DI programs are designed to help replace our intuition about what works and whether we are teaching well with a much more reliable guide: scientific evidence from the classroom.

Science has shown that the mind often does not know how it knows things, nor can it recall how it learned what it knows, much less teach what it knows to others. We *think* we know, but our explanations when tested turn out to be false. Thus, blind people used to give many different explanations for how they managed to avoid bumping into things. Some said they sensed walls through vibrations in their fingertips, others from a tingling in their forehead; still others said they could smell walls. They were confident they knew the mechanism—but in fact they *didn't* know. Every hypothesis but one when tested proved false. Plug up their ears and blind people—*all* blind people—will bump into walls. They do not have different learning styles. Intuition has persuaded them otherwise, but scientific experiments conclusively demonstrate that the blind *hear* walls—the sounds bouncing off of walls—sort of like bats.

> Teachers often think that they're doing what works and that they have evidence to prove it. But self-perception is not the same as independent assessment based on science. DI programs, forged and proven by the scientific method, give teachers a more honest gauge of how much their students are learning and clear benchmarks with which to compare their performance.

So it is with teaching children. Teachers often think that they're doing what works and that they have evidence to prove it. But self-perception is not the same as independent assessment based on science. DI programs, forged and proven by the scientific method, give teachers a more honest gauge of how much their students are learning and clear benchmarks with which to compare their performance.

Engelmann's standard for performance is high: a DI program is never published until even the lowest performing students who go through it in a field test perform 90% or better on the skills taught in the program. If they don't, Engelmann assumes he did something wrong.

"If the student hasn't learned, the teacher hasn't taught—that's not a slogan, it's an operating principle," he says. "You cannot fall in love with your own judgment. Every program we've ever done was significantly revised after field testing. The kids teach us how to do it. We let their mistakes show us where we stepped off the wrong side of the boat. Sometimes it's insulting. Here you work your fanny off trying to design this stuff, you present it to the kids, and wham!—no correct answers. That's an insult! *I* wrote it—*you* should get it! Once you get past that, you recognize that it's okay, you're getting information. Every time they make a mistake and you fix it up, you've learned something and improved your teaching."

Good DI teachers are similarly student-centered. "The kids never lie," one veteran DI teacher says. "The information they give you should feel like somebody hitting you with a brick. If it doesn't, you're not teaching—you're just presenting."

> "If the student hasn't learned, the teacher hasn't taught—that's not a slogan, it's an operating principle," Engelmann says. "You cannot fall in love with your own judgment."

The information Engelmann gets from the field tests that shape his programs is exhaustive—a veritable wall of bricks against false assumptions. Data is kept on how many chances per minute students get to respond, their percentage of first-time correct responses, their error patterns, the *think time* they need for different tasks, how many trials they need to master different tasks, how often and at what interval they need to review things so they don't forget them, how much interference they can tolerate while learning a new task (for instance, how facile must students be at reading words before they can think about their meaning at the same time?), and how much their learning rate accelerates as they learn more and more. Extensive data is also kept on teachers: their pace of delivery, how often they praise and correct their students, *how* they correct students and how often their correction procedures are the right ones, and the specific problems they encounter in delivering the program, such as awkward wording or teaching behaviors that are too hard to master and need to be changed.

Much of what Engelmann has learned from this trove of data about how kids react to scientific instruction is counterintuitive, or at least not obvious.

◊ Children with low IQs learn at rates comparable to children with higher IQs when both groups are taught things that are equally unfamiliar to them (nonsense concepts, for example).

◊ Children differ in what they know and like to do, and they learn at different rates, but they do not learn in different ways: the same scientific techniques of instruction induce learning in everyone.

◊ Learning rates change quickly and spectacularly, particularly on tasks that require analogous reasoning. For instance, a child learning to sort and classify things may need 20 tries on the first set of objects before doing it correctly (e.g., Which of these is not a vehicle?). By the fourth set (e.g., Which of these is not an insect?), the child can usually get it on the first try.

◊ Children from middle-class and affluent homes perform no better at many logic and reasoning tasks than do children from poor homes. Engelmann discovered this when testing *Reasoning and Writing*, a six-level program that teaches those skills in elementary and middle school. The more affluent children were better at grammar and story-telling, but not at making clear arguments or drawing conclusions from evidence.

◊ Low performers have much more trouble learning patterns of numbers than random sequences. "Anything that's patterned will *interfere* with their learning," Engelmann says. "If you didn't know that and you tried to teach at-risk kids the associative principle, you wouldn't realize how much more practice they're going to need. If you say to them '8+1, turn it around, 1+8. Your turn: 8+1, turn it around'—they can't do it. Twenty trials later, they still can't do it, whereas the higher performing kids pick up on it in a heartbeat."

◊ Patterns are just one thread in a tapestry of *thousands* of things that we think are obvious but that at-risk children don't understand. For example, third graders when shown a picture of a ship listing to one side do not know which direction the deck chairs will slide.

Indeed almost everything about teaching at-risk children is counterintuitive. Engelmann's early programs, such as *Reasoning and Writing*, had to be rewritten

33

because he assumed the children knew more than they did. "It's so easy to get a false sense of their world," he says. "We started too far ahead. *We* didn't know what things they were going to have trouble with; we only found out by working with them. You need to know, because unless your program anticipates the kinds of mistakes kids make and pre-empts them, and unless it generates some kind of *response* from kids that shows clearly what you have to correct, you're going to go right past each other like trains in the night, and never *really* provide these kids with the information they need. You'll just assume that when they look at you and nod their heads, they really know."

Engelmann's early programs, such as *Reasoning and Writing,* had to be rewritten because he assumed the children knew more than they did. "It's so easy to get a false sense of their world," he says.

CHAPTER V:
PLAYING THE MUSIC

[handwritten margin note: Percentages for basic skills lower than Percentages for higher order skills "cognitive skills" Technical Report — Wes Becker + Zig for FT]

With DI, Smart Kids Learn Fast Too

Engelmann's programs are so carefully designed to reach the hard-to-teach that even his admirers often miss how well they teach everyone else. Likewise they are so good at teaching basic skills that few teachers appreciate how well they teach the more-advanced knowledge a literate society demands.

A recent major review of the research literature found that Direct Instruction is in fact similarly effective for students whether they are in regular education, special ed, elementary school or high school. The review also found DI to be similarly effective at teaching both early reading skills *and* high-level comprehension. No other method of instruction showed such consistently strong effects with students of different ability levels and ages, and with different subject matters. (The review, *Visible learning: A synthesis of over 800 meta-analyses relating to achievement*, by John Hattie of University of Auckland in New Zealand, was published by Routledge in 2009.)

The federal Follow Through study, which looked at young at-risk children, found that the biggest differences separating DI (the only effective model) from the 21 other models was not on rote learning but on cognitive higher order skills. Forty years later and on the other end of the curve, in Gering, Nebraska, a rural district which uses DI, elementary students classified as gifted are out-performing their gifted peers in non-DI schools in the rest of the state. They have learned so much that Gering's junior high has had to rewrite its curriculum for them, raising standards to make it more like high school.

> A recent major review of the research literature found that Direct Instruction is in fact similarly effective for students whether they are in regular education, special ed, elementary school or high school.

Any teacher flipping through Engelmann's lesson plans would see that they tackle sophisticated skills page after page and are content-rich.

The upper levels of *Reading Mastery* focus on great literature, such as Mark

35

Twain, Nathaniel Hawthorne and Jack London. Earlier levels focus on non-fiction, and contain many things DI teachers confess they themselves never learned. Third graders read about Nancy who becomes less than 1 centimeter tall. Before reading the story, they are taught the science concepts that enable them to predict what will happen when she falls from a counter (she won't get hurt), what problems she will have drinking water (because of the surface tension of a drop of water), and why her voice changed so that her mother could not hear her when she called. In the context of other selections, children learn how rivers change their course and why tire tracks are visible on the road after it rains. They learn the principles of convection and propulsion. They learn Archimedes' law of buoyancy. They learn the difference between induction and deduction, similes and metaphors, and (often mistaught!) facts and opinions.

> In Gering, Nebraska, a rural district which uses DI, elementary students classified as gifted are out-performing their gifted peers in non-DI schools in the rest of the state. They have learned so much that Gering's junior high has had to rewrite its curriculum for them, raising standards to make it more like high school.

Reasoning and Writing teaches how to identify misleading claims in advertising and to draw appropriate conclusions from evidence. *Essentials for Writing* (for middle and high school) teaches the principles of argument and debate. *Corrective Reading* (a remedial program for students who are behind) teaches economic principles and how to apply them. *Morphographic Spelling* teaches rules and techniques for analyzing word parts that most adults do not know. For instance, when trying to spell and understand words like *inspect* and *spectacle*, students learn that *spect* is a morphograph—a word part—that means "to look." (Teachers trained in the program learn that the *rrh* in hemorrhage, rhinorrhea, diarrhea and gonorrhea, means "to flow.")

Many DI teachers and program authors use the programs to teach their own children, often against the advice of their peers, who warn that they will ruin their kids by pushing them too hard.

Jean Osborn, co-founder of the Bereiter-Engelmann preschool and co-author of several programs, including *Language for Learning*, taught her daughter to read with DI when she was four. "By kindergarten she was a good reader," Osborn says. "I always like to say to people who say that DI ruins children: Emily learned to read with DI, she got a PhD at Stanford in history, and she's a professor at University of Chicago. Did DI ruin her life? Of course not."

Emily recalls liking the lessons so much she would try to teach them to the dog. "My life is reading now," she says. "I read and write. That's how I make my living. My mom's regret is she didn't do DI math with me. I'm terrible at math. I have a seven-month-old. I will absolutely teach him with DI. And I will do math with him too."

Bernadette Kelly, a teacher and co-author of DI math programs, moved to Eugene from England just to study with Engelmann. She says her children skipped kindergarten because she had taught them with DI. "I couldn't have done it with any other program," she says. "With smart kids you go fast, you respond to their performance, you skip some of the examples—but they still need careful instruction."

Lindsay Boorman, whose mom used DI with her through sixth grade, graduated from high school at 16, went to college and law school, served as an assistant district attorney in Manhattan, then went to work with her mom,

Emily recalls liking the lessons so much she would try to teach them to the dog. "My life is reading now," she says. "I read and write. That's how I make my living. My mom's regret is she didn't do DI math with me. I'm terrible at math. I have a seven-month-old. I will absolutely teach him with DI. And I will do math with him too."

who runs a DI training company. She says she used DI techniques to prepare for the bar exam (which she passed on the first try), just as she used them to master helping verbs in eighth grade. "That's just how I learn now—it's the quickest way to master something," she says. "If you've done DI enough, you know when you know and you know when you don't know. I know when I've mastered something and when I haven't. It makes me more efficient."

But it's more than about efficiency. Boorman's husband, a policeman, wants their baby girl to share her love of learning. "I got that from DI," she says. "It made me successful. I started reading when I was three. Everyone thought that was marvelous. I'm still an avid reader."

She recalls meeting Engelmann: "It was at a party in Vermont. We were sitting on the back stairs by ourselves. I was four. He asked me if I would read to him. So I read to him—*for an hour*. He was just enthralled. It was like I was playing him music, like I was doing something no one else had ever done. I'll never forget it. He made me feel like the most special person in the world."

CHAPTER VI:
REPUTATION AND MONEY

Why So Few Educators Have Taken Up Engelmann's Programs

DI is the ugly duckling of education, despised and defamed despite repeated demonstrations that it works. No other educational reform strays further from accepted theory, differs more from accepted practice, or draws such brutal slander for its achievements. Engelmann, who can be combative and undiplomatic, has spent 40 years attacking the educational system as an obsolete sham, especially for the poor, and the system has paid him back with vilification and contempt. His programs are shunned by those whose ideas and products they challenge, and misunderstood by those who lack the time or desire to learn how they work. They require training of a kind that few colleges offer and that few working teachers are given the chance to go get. As a result they are little used, except in special education or as an extraordinary intervention, when students' needs are dire and there is pressure to show results.

> DI is the ugly duckling of education, despised and defamed despite repeated demonstrations that it works. No other educational reform strays further from accepted theory, differs more from accepted practice, or draws such brutal slander for its achievements.

DI is unpopular for three reasons: it puts more responsibility on educators to achieve results, it gives teachers less freedom to do what they want in the classroom, and it defies a vast system's enormous stake in the conventional wisdom.

Central to the prevailing view in education is the belief that children learn naturally, and that they learn most when they are allowed to direct the pace and content of their own learning. The ideal teacher is not a teacher at all but "a guide on the side"—a coach who facilitates the child's pre-ordained rate of growth and private creation of knowledge. From these premises flow a host of others. Pre-K and kindergarten teachers are taught that it is not *developmentally appropriate* to seat children at desks, give them worksheets, make them work to learn the alphabet, letter sounds, and math, or assess their academic skills. Teachers in all grades are warned that it is unjust and harmful to group students by skill level to instruct them in skills (because all children are equal and because children learn as much from one another as they do from adults). Math teachers are taught that kids will like math better and be better at it if they are made to figure out their own strategies to solve problems, rather than learn standard procedures from the teacher.

Engelmann's methods explode this entire constellation of myth: children do not construct their own reality about subject matters; teachers need not wait for children to reach a certain age or stage of development before teaching them certain concepts; children do not learn more when teachers teach them less.

Rather than abandon their beliefs (and the lucrative investment in textbooks, training and curricula that express them), rather than honestly examine Engelmann's ideas and methods, DI's detractors have manufactured another stock of myths to justify their rejection of DI.

◊ They say DI does not teach higher order skills—reading comprehension, for example, or algebra (of course, many of DI's curricula are designed to do just that, and Engelmann can prove that they work).

◊ They say DI uses "drill and kill" methods that destroy the love of learning (a visit to a DI class is enough to discredit this claim).

39

◊ They say DI ignores individual differences among students (but in fact Engelmann can specifically demonstrate that DI works for all kinds of students).

◊ They say DI only works for low performers and the poor, not the gifted and the middle class (again, disproved by tests and studies and by simple logic: methods that work for low performers will work for high performers—it's the reverse that's not true).

◊ They say DI turns little kids into robots (certainly not evident in class!) and older boys into criminals (a discredited claim instigated by the author of a rival program).

Engelmann's success also discredits another popular myth: that teachers always know best how to teach their kids, hence should be given wide latitude in the classroom. Critics say the scripted presentations limit teacher creativity and can become boring to teach. But in fact Engelmann's programs are designed to free teachers from having to reinvent the wheel for every class and subject, and to let them focus on the give-and-take with students—which is rarely boring or predictable. Many teachers are relieved that they don't have to be responsible for course design and lesson plans, on top of all their duties in the classroom.

> "DI frees you up to do the fun stuff," says one teacher. "If you're a creative person, you can be creative with DI," says another. "I was creative for 17 years. But I wasn't reaching all my students until I had this structure."

"DI frees you up to do the fun stuff," says one teacher. "If you're a creative person, you can be creative with DI," says another. "I was creative for 17 years. But I wasn't reaching all my students until I had this structure."

And of course DI teachers get to experience that ultimate reward, the thing that makes it all worthwhile, the reason they became teachers in the first place: the success, trust, and indeed love of their students.

No amount of data or teacher testimonial has been able to stop the criticisms of DI or the flow of dollars—billions of taxpayer dollars—to the critics and their own doctrines about how kids learn. This despite the fact that the critics have no scientific backing or proof that their own methods work—quite the opposite: fifty years of lagging student achievement in America has proven their ideas to be failures.

Engelmann thinks the education system needs improvement, but he thinks reforms such as "No Child Left Behind" are doomed to fail because they don't reflect, much less require, any technical understanding of what goes on in the classroom; hence they cannot really evaluate the success or failure of teaching methods. "If you come in with anything that has specifics and requires technical training and objective, easily identified criteria, educators will oppose it," he says. It's as if a team of civil engineers were trying to build a bridge across a deep canyon but refused to use steel beams or an architect's plan to show how they should be put together.

"You can walk into a Direct Instruction classroom and tell right away if anything's wrong. You can see whether the teacher is doing it the right way, whether the kids are placed right. It is all very obvious," Engelmann says. "And that is absolutely opposed to the educational idioms of the last fifty years, which consist mostly of slogans that are hurled about but that do not reduce into precise behaviors about what anybody should do."

No amount of data or teacher testimonial has been able to stop the criticisms of DI or the flow of dollars—billions of taxpayer dollars—to the critics and their own doctrines about how kids learn. This despite the fact that the critics have no scientific backing or proof that their own methods work—quite the opposite: fifty years of lagging student achievement in America has proven their ideas to be failures.

CHAPTER VII: INCONVENIENT TRUTHS

Bad Programs Cause Most Learning Failures

Engelmann says his critics fail to understand or accept a whole set of hard truths about teaching and learning. Engelmann discovered these truths through years of trial and error in the classroom; he tried the easier, more conventional ways to teach, but he kept running into inconvenient facts: the easier ways didn't work!

Writing programs is hard. A talented DI author and Engelmann protégée once worked 17 hours to design a five-minute sequence to teach a single concept to mastery. Her struggles are typical. Designing clear instruction is a peculiar skill that almost nobody does well and that almost everybody (alas!) depends on. There may be a half-dozen ways to do it right, but there are *infinite* ways to get it wrong.

> Asking teachers to design instruction is like asking the pilot of a 747 to design the plane, or the conductor of a symphony to compose the score, or the lead in *Hamlet* to write the play.

"The Wright brothers had to orchestrate a thousand specific details to make a flying machine. If any one of those pieces had been missing or misconstructed or out of place, the machine would have failed," Engelmann says. "So it is with educational programs. The program has to be an orchestration of detail. The teacher works with pitzy, flyspeck details. That's what *we* work with, because we know that unless those details are in place, the students won't learn."

It is unrealistic and unfair to expect teachers to be able to write their own lessons. Asking teachers to design instruction is like asking the pilot of a 747 to design the plane, or the conductor of a symphony to compose the score, or the lead in *Hamlet* to write the play. *Theory of Instruction*, a daunting work few have read, goes on for nearly 400 pages showing how it might be done. John Stuart Mill, Engelmann's intellectual forbearer, takes 645 pages to describe similar ideas in *A System of Logic*, an even denser work published in 1843. Plainly put: it's hard to communicate how to communicate; it's not so clear how to *be clear*. The typical

Engelmann program takes anywhere from three to ten years to develop. Asking teachers to match this effort is unrealistic—they already have a challenging full-time job in the classroom.

Most teachers will teach no better than their program. "Traditional textbooks assume that the teacher is able to explain the material, design some form of tests that reveal what the students learn, and make what is taught today consistent with what will be taught in the future," Engelmann says. "That is an elitist assumption. There is no empirical evidence to suggest that teachers can create effective teaching from text material that is not explicit and carefully sequenced. If there are mistakes in the program, or if the program is vague or leads them to a dead end, they will know something is wrong but they won't know how to fix it. It's not because teachers don't know how to teach. It's because there's a great difference between teaching and designing effective instruction. Most learning failures are caused by bad programs, not bad teachers. No amount of good teaching behavior can bail a teacher out of a bad program. If you want to get mad at somebody, get mad at the people who give you broad-brush strokes about teaching and then leave *you* to figure out the details because *they* don't know how to do it."

Engelmann learned these truths slowly and painfully. When he first began training teachers in his methods, he assumed that what was obvious to him would

be obvious to everyone else and that if he gave some general directions most of them would catch on. He thought scripting the words and examples was unnecessary and wouldn't work.

"At first we had some basic formats that you had to learn in your head. It was a disaster," he says. "We'd demonstrate and give teachers lists of instances, but they couldn't get it. We had to correct virtually everything. They didn't know what examples to use, how many examples, in what sequence. They didn't know what problem types to avoid. These were smart teachers. It was just foreign to them. They couldn't go ten seconds without making a mistake.

"Most learning failures are caused by bad programs, not bad teachers."

"So we tried a global script. We formatted the curricula with general guidelines, showing the problem types you'd put on the board and a rough indication of the wording. That didn't work either. Teachers don't realize how much they over-talk, how often their instructions are unclear, and how impatient they get with the kids when they're unable to respond exactly the way they want. Consistency in wording is necessary, especially for low performers. You can't get far without it. And we found we couldn't get consistency in wording or praise unless we scripted the presentation. So we bit the bullet. Once we did that we could preempt all kinds of problems and train new people. Teachers could do the programs quite well and generalize to other things.

"At first teachers think the script is confining. Most of them come around when they see how well it works for their kids."

CHAPTER VIII:
BETTING ON SCIENCE

Will Anybody Take Engelmann's $100,000 Offer?

Engelmann's curricula are as numerous and varied as the challenges they are designed to help teachers overcome. He has written programs to teach reading, oral language development, reasoning, and arithmetic to preschoolers; those subjects plus spelling, cursive handwriting, expository and narrative writing, and physical and earth science for children in elementary school; pre-algebra and writing to meet state test requirements for middle and high school; remedial programs in the core subjects for students who have fallen behind and for adults out of school; oral language for students learning English; and a *Low Performers Manual* for students with autism, memory loss, and other problems.

He has published a memory building program, *Your World of Facts*, which uses a game format to teach useful background knowledge. *Reasoning and Writing* teaches logic. (There might be fewer fads and erroneous theories in education had more people gone through *Reasoning and Writing*: we would have been trained to pick apart their faulty premises.) He has designed instructional sequences that help young children learn to tie their shoes, brain-trauma victims to relearn their own names and to speak, deaf mutes to learn language via vibration patterns transmitted to the skin. He has created step-by-step instructions to get autistics to stop shredding their bedclothes (a not uncommon behavior). He has written two best-selling books for parents—*Give Your Child a Superior Mind* and *Teach Your Child to Read in 100 Easy Lessons*—plus many more professional books, chapters and monographs, and more than 100 articles. He has co-authored three computer programs—the *Funnix* series—that teach beginning reading and math, and that are designed so parents can use them with no training. Resolute and keen-minded in his old age (he turns 80 in November), he has published three major programs in the last year—*Essentials for Writing* and *Essentials for Algebra* for secondary school students and *Direct Instruction Spoken English* for students in second grade or above who speak no English. He writes six hours a day.

In his younger days, Engelmann traveled the country demonstrating how DI works. He would go into schools, prisons and hospitals, ask to see their toughest cases, and promptly teach them what no one else thought they would ever learn. Stories of miracles abound. He prompted an autistic 15-year-old girl to respond for the first time in her life. He got a seven-year-old boy who had never spoken to say five words in half an hour. He coached a phobic child over his terror of tricycles. He got a group of unruly six-year-olds to work hard by rewarding them with gravel from the school parking lot. He taught inner-city preschool kids complex fractions. He taught children who didn't know the word *is* to speak in complete sentences, understand opposites and count to ten. He got illiterate gang leaders to enforce good behavior in a remedial reading class (he also taught them to read). But these were not really miracles. They were artful applications of his theory, no more miraculous than a missile in flight.

For forty years Engelmann has offered to bet anyone $100,000 that he or anyone trained to use his programs could out-teach anyone else using any other approach. No one has ever taken the bet. Based on the evidence that has been amassed showing how well DI works, anyone who did would have to be considered the underdog.

For forty years Engelmann has offered to bet anyone $100,000 that he or anyone trained to use his programs could out-teach anyone else using any other approach. No one has ever taken the bet.

Project Follow Through, the government study that examined 22 methods of instruction and found Direct Instruction worked best by far, tracked more than 75,000 at-risk students in 170 communities from kindergarten through the end of third grade. Students were tested on language skills, reading, spelling, and math. DI students did best in all four subjects. They also scored highest on tests designed to gauge their self-image and sense of responsibility. More than a hundred studies and meta-analyses since Follow Through (including fifteen in the last three years and 75 in the last decade) have confirmed various aspects of its findings and found that DI accelerates learning in older students, children with above-average IQs, different racial and ethnic groups, students with disabilities and in special education, and students in urban, rural and suburban schools. The research has also found that DI raises the rates at which students graduate from high school and go to college, and lowers rates of grade-retention, discipline problems and referrals to special ed—all benefits that have been found to save money. No scientific study has found negative effects from DI. Such consistency of results across populations and settings is rare in the social sciences.

CHAPTER IX: GREAT TEACHERS

Passion and Persistence

In a field known more for its fashions than stability, DI hasn't changed much in 40 years. It treats teachers as professionals and has remained true to everything they say they want for their students. It differentiates instruction. It encourages participation and feedback. It builds self-esteem, self-reliance and self-control. It rewards perseverance, honors high expectations and respects diversity. It shuns labels. It makes learning fun. It is rocket fuel for the gifted and a lifeline for the poor.

DI teachers remain a special breed. They see the world through Engelmann's eyes because they believe they have found a teaching method that *works* where countless others have failed. Like all good teachers, they tend to be smart, inquisitive, enterprising and methodical; earnest, persistent, confident, and proud. They feel the urgency of their jobs. They know there is nothing DI teaches that their kids do not desperately need to know, and they blame themselves if their kids fail to learn it. They believe they can teach anybody. They like teaching the hard-to-teach as much or more than the gifted. They are ambitious to be the best. When praised, they are bothered if others fail to understand that it's not just *them*, it's the program.

> DI differentiates instruction. It encourages participation and feedback. It builds self-esteem, self-reliance and self-control. It rewards perseverance, honors high expectations and respects diversity. It shuns labels. It makes learning fun. It is rocket fuel for the gifted and a lifeline for the poor.

Above all, DI teachers cherish the deep bonds of affection DI inspires in their students, many of whom experience success for the first time thanks to their teaching. Far from alienating kids, DI makes teachers more pleasing to their students, even as it makes students more pleasing to their teachers, who take pride in their growth, and indeed grow with them.

Detractors say DI gets boring to teach, but a good DI teacher rarely gets bored.

"If you're bored teaching an effective program, that's a red flag," one DI trainer says. "It means you're not in the kid's head. You're focused on presenting the curriculum. If you have walked the bridge from presenting to teaching, then teaching never gets boring because a kid can make a mistake in a million different ways. *That's* what's exciting about teaching and what DI helps you deal with."

"I can give good feedback with DI," a young teacher agrees. "In other programs, I don't know where to begin."

Fixing the variety of mistakes kids make is also what makes teaching so hard, even with DI. "If you know how to do this, you *can* do remarkable things," Engelmann says. "You can turn around kids nobody else can teach. But you have to know *technically* how to do it. And it's really frustrating because, God, so much of the stuff we do so few people understand. I don't want to go to the grave not passing this on to someone else."

Most people who use Engelmann's programs buy them from commercial distributors and don't actually know who he is, so they don't see how their success is connected to his passion. He hates to give up on a problem. He once worked for two months trying to get an elderly stroke victim to speak a single word. He ran thousands of trials testing a tool to help the deaf. He deciphered a Mayan text that had gone unsolved for centuries. Science is what moves him. He drops schools when they stray from the scientific techniques he invented, and he'll help willing people who lack means for free. He plants trees because he likes to make things grow. He began painting watercolors as anger management after he wrote an angry book, *War Against the Schools' Academic Child Abuse*. In his younger days, he collected motorcycles.

Engelmann's grandmother used to call him the wunderkind. His mark on edu-

cation, though it might have been larger, has not been slight. He analyzed three of the most complex subjects—oral language development, writing and math—and created the tools to teach them systematically, even to low performers. He made educators aware of the importance of curriculum. He showed that poor and disabled children can learn at reasonable rates using standard levels of funding, and that it is therefore fair that we hold ourselves accountable for their learning. He showed that student behavior is inseparable from instruction: the better the instruction, the better students behave. He showed that teacher quality is inseparable from curriculum: the better the program, the better teachers teach. He disproved the stereotype that learning must be painful and full of furrowed brows: good instruction turns learning into a game students can win. He showed that poor kids need good instruction year after year to catch up to their peers.

Too many four-year-olds don't know how to speak. Too many teenagers don't know how to write a sentence. Too many adults don't know math. Engelmann has taken the measure of our nation. He has shown us precisely what we need to know, and he has figured out a good way to teach us. What he does not know, and what no one knows, is how to convince us. The science he invented has not been refuted. It's been banished and ignored. The republic survives, but Engelmann has given us a tantalizing look at how much better we all might be. Even as we ignore him, he persists with his full-throated cry: Teachers, you can do this! You can teach the poor! You can lift this nation! And he persists with what he loves and does best: writing programs to show us how we might reach our lofty goals.

49

APPENDIX I:
REINFORCING SUCCESS

Snapshot of a DI Class

Stephanie Brown has taught Direct Instruction math, reading, and language programs in Baltimore for thirteen years, the last eight in all-day, state-funded pre-K at Hampstead Hill Academy, a public charter school. Typically 80% of her students come from poor homes, more than half are African-American or Latino, and one-third are immigrants still learning English. Many arrive not knowing how to hold a pair of scissors, use pronouns, speak in complete sentences, or follow simple directions. By the end of the school year, they have learned to sort objects into classes, identify opposites, recognize logical absurdities, use synonyms and if/then statements, create definitions for objects, read simple sentences, and do simple addition problems.

In the first months of school, Brown teaches her four-year-olds to sit at desks, work independently on exercises with pencil and paper, and concentrate for up to 30 minutes at a stretch (twice each morning) as she delivers the fast-paced DI lessons, one each for language and math. During DI time she breaks the class into three groups, arranged by skill level, to teach them more efficiently. She praises students by name when they answer questions correctly, rewards them for good behavior, and corrects their mistakes quickly, firmly and consistently. Every one of these practices—standard DI operating procedure—breaks the established rules of early childhood education, Brown's accredited field.

"We're going to start off with something really hard, but I think you can do it," Brown says, beginning a lesson from Engelmann's *Distar Arithmetic* program. Seven children sit in a semicircle around her. Nine others are at their desks, cutting out, coloring, and ordering the pictures of the life stages of a butterfly. Two others get extra practice on a language lesson with Ms. Brown's assistant near the door. It is early June.

"Read this," Brown says, pointing at the "+2" written on the blackboard. "Everyone, get ready…" Following the script, she signals with her hand, and seven voices in unison say: "Plus two!" The simultaneity of response, a feature of all DI programs, instantly lets her know whether all her students are learning what she is trying to teach without having to take the time to call on each one individually.

"Very good! *Plus two* means the number that is two more. So, four plus two equals what number? Everyone…"

"Six!" they all shout.

The children write in their workbooks the answer to the problems that are on the blackboard above a number line: 6 + 2, 3 + 2 and 7 + 2. Ms. Brown quickly checks their answers and says, "I don't see any backwards numbers. Very good!"

The lesson lasts 20 minutes, after which the children return to their desks and five others take their place for a lesson from *Language for Thinking*, another DI curriculum. The transition takes no more than a minute. Each DI lesson reinforces and extends several strands of knowledge and skills that the children have learned in earlier lessons. Today's lesson includes work on the calendar, verb tenses, absurdities, questioning skills, definitions, opposites, and articulating descriptions and taking physical actions.

"We're going to talk about today, tomorrow, and one week from today," Brown says. "Tell me the day of the week it is today. Get ready…"

"Tuesday."

"Tell me the day of the week it will be tomorrow."

"Wednesday."

"Tell me the day of the week it will be one week from today."

"Tuesday."

Pointing to a calendar, Brown says, "Tell me tomorrow's date. Think. (*She pauses to give them think time.*) Get ready…"

"June 3rd."

Detecting some confusion, she repeats the right answer and has the children repeat it before moving on.

"How many months are in a year?"

"Twelve."

"Say the fact."

"There are twelve months in a year."

"Say the months."

The group chants them in unison.

Moving from facts to can/do statements, Brown says, "Get ready to answer some questions about a pair of scissors. Can you use a pair of scissors to cut paper?"

"Yes!"

"Can you use a pair of scissors to cut string?"

"Yes!"

"Can you tear scissors into little pieces?"

(Laughter) "No!"

"Can you drink from a pair of scissors?"

(More laughter) "No!"

"Can you put a pair of scissors in a box?"

"Yes."

"Can you cook hamburgers with a pair of scissors?"

"No!"

"Can you step on a pair of scissors?"

"Yes!"

"Can you hide in a pair of scissors?"

(Loud laughter) "No!"

"Listen to this story and figure out what's wrong with it. There was a woman. She wanted to wash the dishes, so she got out a broom."

She calls on a little girl who points out the absurdity.

"A monkey walked in the rain. He wore a bathing suit so that he wouldn't get wet. What's wrong with that story?"

Laughter and a series of right answers.

Moving to verb tenses, she says, "The baby will cry. Does that statement tell what the baby *did* or what the baby *will do*?"

"What the baby *will do*!"

The lesson ends with Brown leading the children step-by-step in the formation of definitions. "A hat is clothing you wear on your head," one student says. "A scarf is clothing you wear on your neck," says another, very slowly.

> "The children aren't stressed out—they feel like the smartest kids on the planet," Brown says. "Even the ones with behavior problems—it settles them."

The least advanced group, the Bananas, comes up for a lesson in *Language for Learning*, the program Engelmann wrote to address the language deficit in poor children. The focus today is on calendar facts, opposites, and similarities.

"The sheep were very slow," Brown says. "Now say the sentence that tells the opposite about the sheep."

"The sheep were very fast."

"The story made us feel sad. Now say the sentence that tells the opposite."

"The story made us feel happy."

"I'm thinking of a broom and a hammer. How are they the same?"

One girl answers: "They both have handles."

"Yes. Very good. They both have handles," Brown says. "Here's another way they're the same: they both help you do work. Ok. How are they *different*?"

A boy says: "A hammer hurts you when it hits you and a broom doesn't."

Brown does DI lessons in the morning when the children are fresh. The rest of the day is devoted to standard pre-K fare: art, music, free play, gym, story time, and theme-based centers where students get to choose their activities, such as playing with blocks or kitchen utensils.

"The children aren't stressed out—they feel like the smartest kids on the planet," Brown says. "Even the ones with behavior problems—it settles them."

APPENDIX II: RESEARCH ON DIRECT INSTRUCTION

Meta-Analyses and Synthesis of Research

Over the last 25 years several researchers have reviewed and summarized the vast literature on Direct Instruction, many using meta-analysis. Meta-analysis is the statistical analysis of a group of previous studies pertaining to a given intervention. The effect size for a teaching methodology reflects the gain in learning produced by the methodology expressed in standard deviation units. Effect sizes are typically based on comparisons to previous outcomes with the same group or outcomes attained during the same time period by a comparison group. An effect of 0.25 or greater is generally said to represent an educationally significant gain or difference.

Adams, G., & Engelmann, S. (1996). *Research on Direct Instruction: 25 years beyond DISTAR*. Seattle, WA: Educational Achievement Systems.
Adams and Engelmann's meta-analysis of 34 selected studies found an average effect size of 0.97 per variable studied for Direct Instruction—an indication that it was highly effective.

Borman, G.D., Hewes, G.M., Overman, L.T., & Brown, S. (2003). Comprehensive school reform and achievement: A meta-analysis. *Review of Educational Research, 73(2)*, 125-230.
Borman, Hewes, Overman, and Brown examined studies pertaining to 29 comprehensive school reform models. Among the interventions categorized as having the "strongest evidence of effectiveness" (Direct Instruction, School Development Program, and Success for All), Direct Instruction was found to have the largest average effect size (0.21) and to be grounded in the greatest number of studies—49 studies containing a total of 182 comparisons. The remaining interventions were generally based on less rigorous evidence and fewer studies, and were found to produce widely varying effect sizes.

Hattie, J. (2009). *Visible learning: A synthesis of over 800 meta-analyses relating to achievement.* **London and New York: Routledge.**

Hattie synthesized the results of previous meta-analyses of various factors that have been investigated with regard to effects on student achievement. Direct Instruction was found to be one of the most effective teaching strategies. Four meta-analyses that included DI were examined. Across 304 studies, 597 effects, and over 42,000 students, he found an average effect size of 0.59 with similar positive results (0.99) for both regular and special education students.

Przychodzin-Havis, A. M., Marchand-Martella, N. E., Martella, R. C., & Azim, D. (2004). Direct Instruction mathematics programs: An overview and research summary. *Journal of Direct Instruction, 4(1),* **53-84.**

The authors reviewed twelve studies of Direct Instruction in mathematics and found significant results favoring DI in eleven of the twelve.

Przychodzin-Havis, A. M., Marchand-Martella, N. E., Martella, R. C., Miller, D. A., Warner, L., Leonard, B., & Chapman, S. (2005). An analysis of Corrective Reading research. *Journal of Direct Instruction, 5(1),* **37-65.**

The authors reviewed 28 studies and found positive results for Direct Instruction, Corrective Reading in 26 of them.

Schieffer, C., Marchand-Martella, N. E., Martella, R. C., Simonsen, F. L., & Waldron-Soler, K. M. (2002). An analysis of the Reading Mastery program: Effective components and research review. *Journal of Direct Instruction, 2(2),* **87-119.**

A comprehensive research review of 25 published studies and two large-scale research reviews found results strongly favoring Direct Instruction's Reading Mastery program. Two thirds of the studies reported significant results favoring Reading Mastery/DISTAR Reading, one fifth reported no significant differences, and approximately one seventh (14%) had findings that favored the comparison programs.

What Works Clearinghouse. (2007). *Beginning reading topic report.* **Washington, DC: U.S. Department of Education. Retrieved September 20, 2011, from www.education-consumers.org/WWC_read.pdf**

In contrast to the several syntheses and meta-analyses noted above, the US Department of Education's What Works Clearinghouse (WWC) concluded that there was insufficient evidence to determine whether Direct Instruction was an effective method for teaching beginning reading. The WWC arrived at its conclusion by ruling that almost all of the published studies on beginning reading instruction (not just studies pertaining to DI) were insufficiently rigorous to be included in the WWC review. Of the 887 studies pertaining to beginning reading instruction, only 27 were deemed to have fully met WWC standards. None were studies of Direct Instruction. Among the studies excluded was the federal government's own 10-year-long comparison of all major approaches to teaching at-risk children—the Follow Through project (see chart on page 12). Follow Through (1965-1975), the largest and most comprehensive study of its kind, was disqualified because it was conducted earlier than 1985. The WWC review is generally viewed as a misstep in the ongoing evolution of the WWC as a resource for educators. WWC's reviews provide little useful guidance as to how educators might choose among the widely used reading programs that are supported by published studies that WWC deems to be technically inadequate. References to the changes that have taken place in the WWC assessment processes and critiques of the WWC assessment of beginning reading programs—too numerous to list here—are available through the Education Consumers Foundation at www.education-consumers.org/WWC.html.

White, W. A. T. (1988). A meta-analysis of the effects of Direct Instruction in special education. *Education and Treatment of Children, 11(4)*, **364-374.**

White's (1988) meta-analysis of studies using Direct Instruction with special education populations found an average effect size of 0.84. This study included 12 of the same studies considered in the Adams and Engelmann study, listed above, as well as 13 additional studies, but the results were similar.

Syntheses of Research on Reading Instruction

Two major reviews of reading research sponsored by the federal government do not endorse any specific reading instruction programs; however, they do validate the efficacy of the various practices that are included in Direct Instruction reading programs.

National Reading Panel (2000). *Teaching children to read: An evidence-based assessment of the scientific research literature on reading and its implications for reading instruction.* **Retrieved from   http://www.nichd.nih.gov/publications/ nrp/upload/report.pdf**

Based on a three-year assessment of thousands of studies, a panel of experts convened by the National Institute of Child Health and Human Development found that effective reading programs have certain key features, all of which are core aspects of Direct Instruction. These include systematic and explicit instruction in phonics and phonemic awareness and the use of decodable text and oral practice formats. The report found that repetition and multiple exposures to vocabulary items are important and it confirmed the validity of certain DI techniques to improve comprehension. These include question-answering, in which the reader answers questions posed by the teacher and is given immediate feedback as to correctness, and summarization, where readers are taught to integrate ideas and generalize from the text information.

Snow, C. E., Burns, M. S., & Griffin, P. (Eds.). (1998). *Preventing reading difficulties in young children.* **Washington, DC: National Academy Press.**

The National Reading Council (NRC) report reviewed all of the major studies on reading instruction going back to Chall's 1967 classic, *Learning to Read, The Great Debate*. It affirmed the effectiveness of systematic, code-emphasis programs of direct instruction. In particular, it affirmed the findings of the federal Follow Through project, which had concluded that DI was the only approach, among 22 studied, that accelerated reading achievement in at-risk children. Moreover, the NRC report noted that studies completed subsequent to Follow Through confirmed that the impact of DI on student achievement was long-lasting. In addition, it recommended "Explicit instruction that directs children's attention to the sound structure of oral language and to the connections between speech sounds and spellings" (p. 6). It noted the importance of student motivation and of teaching background knowledge, vocabulary, and "the syntax and rhetorical structures of written language" (p. 6) and recommended "direct instruction about comprehension strategies such as summarizing, predicting, and monitoring" (p. 6)—all features of Engelmann's Direct Instruction.

Project Follow Through:
U.S. Office of Education, 1967-1977

Stebbins, L. B., St. Pierre, R. G., Proper, E. C., Anderson, R. B., & Cerva, T. R. (1977). *Education as experimentation: A planned variation model (Vol IV-A)*. Cambridge, MA: Abt Associates. Retrieved from: http://www.eric.ed.gov/ERIC-WebPortal/search/detailmini.jsp?_nfpb=true&_&ERICExtSearch_Search-Value_0=ED148490&ERICExtSearch_SearchType_0=no&accno=ED148490

Kennedy, M. M. (1978). *Findings from the Follow Through planned variation study*. U.S. Office of Education. Retrieved from: https://www.msu.edu/~mkennedy/publications/docs/Federal%20Programs/Follow%20Through/Kennedy%2078%20FT%20findings.pdf

[handwritten margin note: Researcher says that study directly contradicted what is said on p 35?]

The Follow Through project was designed to be a horse race in which different models for teaching at-risk children would compete under equitable, exacting conditions to see which, if any, would produce student achievement outcomes superior to the norm for at-risk children. Multiple models of teaching were implemented in 51 school districts over a 10-year period. It was the largest educational experiment ever undertaken, and Direct Instruction was the clear winner among the 9 models that completed the project.

For reasons having to do primarily with educational politics, the Follow Through results were never clearly communicated to school districts and Direct Instruction never received the credit it deserved as a vastly superior methodology for improving basic skills with at-risk children. To the contrary, the low-performing models were provided additional funding on the grounds that they had a greater need for improvement, and a number of them were repackaged and remain in use today.

See the figure on page 12 for a summary of the Follow Through outcomes.

The controversy pertaining to the dissemination of the Follow Through outcomes is discussed in the following references:

Carnine, D. W. (1983). Government discrimination against effective educational practices. *Proceedings of the Subcommittee on Human Resources Hearing on Follow Through Amendments of 1983*, 99-103. Wash. D. C.: U. S. Government Printing Office.

Carnine, D. W. (1984). The federal commitment to excellence: Do as I say, not as I do. *Educational Leadership*, 4, 87-88.

Effective School Practices (Volume 15 Number 1, Winter 1995-6): http://darkwing.uoregon.edu/~adiep/ft/151toc.htm. See especially "Follow Through: Why Didn't

We?" by Cathy L. Watkins, California State University-Stanislaus, and "Project Follow Through: In-Depth and Beyond" by Gary Adams, Educational Achievement Systems, Seattle.

Engelmann, S. (2007). *Teaching needy kids in our backward system: 42 years of trying.* Eugene, Oregon: ADI Press.

Recent Studies of Direct Instruction

The meta-analyses and reviews of literature described above provide accumulated evidence of many different studies of Direct Instruction. All of the studies confirm that the effects of DI are positive and strong. Similar results appear with recent work. The examples below involve reading and mathematics, general education and special education students, rural and urban settings, and studies that span one year and those that look at multiple years. All of the results have effect sizes very similar to those found in the meta-analyses.

Carlson, C.D., & Francis, D.J. (2003). Increasing the reading achievement of at-risk children through direct instruction: Evaluation of the Rodeo Institute for Teacher Excellence (RITE). *Journal of Education for Students Placed At Risk, 7(2),* 141-166.

In one of the largest multi-year studies of its type, Carlson and Francis examined the effects of the Direct Instruction-based Rodeo Institute for Teacher Excellence (RITE) program on reading achievement of K-2 students. Effects were measured both yearly and longitudinally across three years. Results indicated that students enrolled in the RITE program consistently outperformed comparison students on standardized reading measures. The study also found that the greater the number of years that students participated in RITE, the more they outperformed comparison students—an indication that the intervention was not transitory or weak on any of the levels of the program. The study involved 9300 students and 277 teachers. All of the outcome measures favored the RITE students, with differences between the intervention and comparison groups growing progressively from K through 2.

Crowe, E. C., Connor, C. M., & Petscher, Y. (2009). Examining the core: Relations among reading curricula, poverty, and first through third grade reading achievement. *Journal of School Psychology, 47,* 187-214.

59

Crowe, Connor, and Petscher compared growth in oral reading skills over one year for students using six different reading curricula: Open Court, Reading Mastery, Harcourt, Houghton Mifflin, Scott Foresman, and Success for All. Over 30,000 students from the state of Florida were included in the analysis. The researchers found that students studying with Reading Mastery had greater growth than students in other curricula, and the effect size for Reading Mastery versus other curricula in first grade was 0.44.

Kamps, D., Abbott, M., Greenwood, C., Wills, H., Veerkamp, M., & Kaufman, J. (2008). Effects of small-group reading instruction and curriculum differences for students most at risk in kindergarten: Two-year results for secondary- and tertiary-level interventions. *Journal of Learning Disabilities, 41(2),* 101-114.

This study focused on 87 students believed to be at risk for reading failure based on demographic characteristics and skills at entry to school. Participants received small-group reading intervention during first and second grades in either Reading Mastery, Early Interventions in Reading, Read Well, or Programmed Reading. Over time students in Reading Mastery had significantly stronger gains (effect size=0.51-0.66) relative to the other three programs.

Stockard, J. (2010). Promoting reading achievement and countering the "Fourth-Grade Slump": The impact of Direct Instruction on reading achievement in fifth grade. *Journal of Education for Students Placed at Risk, 15,* 218-240.

Previous research has documented a substantial decline in standardized test scores of children from low-income backgrounds relative to more advantaged peers in later elementary grades—the so-called "fourth-grade slump." This investigation examined changes in reading achievement from first to fifth grade for students in a large urban school system with a high proportion of economically disadvantaged students. Students were taught reading by Direct Instruction (DI), Open Court, or a mixture of other curricula selected by the individual school. At the outset of the study, the first grade students in the DI schools had lower vocabulary and comprehension scores than students in either of the other two treatment groups. By fifth grade, however, the DI students had the highest vocabulary and comprehension averages—averages that exceeded the fifth grade national average. These impressive results, "suggest that the [DI] curriculum has long-term impacts and, at least for students in this high-poverty school system, can help counter the well documented tendency for declining achievement over time" (p. 234).

Stockard, J. (2010). Improving elementary level mathematics achievement in a large urban district: The effects of Direct Instruction in the Baltimore City Public School System. *Journal of Direct Instruction, 10,* 1-16.

From 1998 to 2003, selected schools in the Baltimore City Public School System (BCPSS) taught mathematics using Direct Instruction. This report compared math achievement for schools using DI with similar schools in the system. First grade students who received Direct Instruction had significantly higher levels of achievement on the Comprehensive Test of Basic Skills (CTBS) subtests of mathematics computations (effect size = .25) and mathematics concepts and applications (effect size = .32; n > 40,000). Among the students who began first grade in the BCPSS and remained in the same schools five years later as fifth graders (n> 4,000), those who had received Direct Instruction as first graders had significantly higher scores on the measure of mathematics concepts and applications than students attending the other schools.

Stockard, J. (2011). Increasing reading skills in rural areas: An analysis of three school districts. *Journal of Research in Rural Education, 26(8),* 1-19. **Retrieved from http://jrre.psu.edu/articles/26-8.pdf**

In a study of 1600 students attending schools in rural Midwestern districts, Stockard examined the changes in reading skills brought about by the Direct Instruction Reading Mastery program. Students who received the DI curriculum from the beginning of kindergarten (full exposure cohorts) were compared to those who began the curriculum in later grades. Those in the full exposure cohorts had significantly higher reading skills than students in the other cohorts, and their scores were at or above national averages. In the one district for which scores on a statewide reading assessment were available, the percentage of students scoring at a high level went from well below the state average to above the state average in the five years of the study (effect size = .31).

APPENDIX III: CONTROVERSIAL FINDINGS

Citing an individual study to prove that Direct Instruction doesn't work is like citing a rainstorm in Tucson to prove that southern Arizona isn't a desert. The preponderance of evidence shows otherwise. Hundreds of studies over 40 years have shown DI to be highly beneficial for a broad range of students; however, there have been two reports of negative findings that appear to show the contrary, and both of them were sensationalized in the media. Neither report is credible and both have been discounted, but both are addressed below in the interest of providing a full account of the evidence pertaining to DI.

Schweinhart, L. J., Weikart, D. P., & Larner, M. B. (1986). Consequences of three preschool curriculum models through age 15. *Early Childhood Research Quarterly, 1(1)*, 15-45.

Schweinhart, Weikart, and Larner suggested that the higher rate of juvenile delinquency found in a group of 15-year-olds was the consequence of their exposure to Direct Instruction as 4-year-olds. A nine-page article contesting these findings was published in a later issue of the same journal. (See Gersten, R. [1986]. Response to "Consequences of three preschool curriculum models through age 15." *Early Childhood Research Quarterly, 1*, 293-302.)

Schweinhart and his colleagues compared 3 groups of 18 youth who had attended a DI program, the author's Perry Preschool/High Scope program, or a traditional nursery school. They found a marginally higher percentage of self-reported juvenile delinquency among the alumni of the DI group.

No study prior to or following the Schweinhart, Weikart, and Larner report found a similar result. To the contrary, a 2002 study of long-term outcomes for 171 children who had been randomly assigned to either a DI or cognitively-oriented preschool found no differences in juvenile delinquency between the two groups at age 15. (See Mills, P. E., Cole, K. N., Jenkins, J. R., & Dale, P. S. [2002, Fall]. Early exposure to Direct Instruction and subsequent juvenile delinquency: A prospective examination. *Exceptional Children, 69[1]*, 85-96. Retrieved from http://www.adihome.org/articles/JDI_03_01_04.pdf)

The Schweinhart, Weikart, and Larner article might have been ignored had it not been for a New York Times article that highlighted its findings. (See Hechinger, F. M. [1986, April 22]. Preschool programs. *The New York Times*. Retrieved from http://www.nytimes.com/1986/04/22/science/about-education-preschool-programs.html) Columnist Fred Hechinger quoted High/Scope Foundation President and co-author David Weikart regarding the "dangers" of DI and its "pressure cooker" approach. The High/Scope preschool model was Direct Instruction's principal competitor for federal funding at the time. Following Hechinger's report, the Schweinhart, Weikart, and Larner study was cited hundreds of times in the academic literature, and today it generates thousands of hits on Google. For many readers, their only exposure to the term *Direct Instruction* has been in conjunction with the Hechinger article and its fallout. The fact that the study by Mills, Cole, Jenkins, and Dale was unable to replicate the findings of Schweinhart, Weikart, and Larner has received little media attention.

Ryder, R.J., Sekulski, J., & Silberg, A. (2003). *Results of Direct Instruction reading program evaluation longitudinal results: First through third grade 2000-2003.* Milwaukee, WI: School of Education.

Another report that has received much media attention claimed that DI was less effective than "traditional instruction" in teaching reading to first through third-grade students in two Wisconsin districts, one urban, one suburban, over a three-year period. This study, too, might have received little scholarly attention had the authors not held a press conference to announce their findings and promote them in the media.

The study had been requested by a state legislator and was funded by a state grant. Its administration was plagued with problems from the start. The first author took over the project after the principal investigator resigned. Only 80 of 224 students enrolled in Year 1 of the study remained at the end; and because of administrative changes made during the course of the study, no one knew for sure how many, if any, received DI exclusively throughout the course of the three-year investigation.

Published online in January, 2004, the Ryder, Sekulski, and Silberg study was attacked by scholars within days of its publication. A peer reviewed response was published later in the same year. (See Adams, G. L., & Slocum, T. A. [with Railsback, G.L., Gallagher, S.A., McCright, S.A., Uchytil, R.A., Conlon, W.W., & Davis, J.T.]. [2004]. A critical review of Randall Ryder 's report of Direct Instruction reading in two Wisconsin school districts. *Journal of Direct Instruction, 4[2]*, 111-127.)

Citing a host of problems, the authors asked ". . . how a report with so many serious flaws could be published and taken seriously by the educational community" (p. 126). They also called for a review by the American Educational Research Association.

A subsequent peer-reviewed report based on the same data was published by Ryder, Burton, and Silberg in 2006. (See Ryder, R. J., Burton, J. L., & Silberg, A. [2006]. Longitudinal study of Direct Instruction effects from first through third grades. *Journal of Educational Research, 99 [3]*, 179-191.) It reached somewhat different statistical conclusions than those stated in the original online version but suffered from most of the same flaws that were in the original report.

The most serious problem was a lack of clarity with respect to exactly what treatment was received by the various groups of students. In the urban school system, the DI group included a school that used Reading Mastery and another school that "used a mixed-method approach in which teachers determined the extent to which DI and other instructional methods were used" (Ryder et al., 2006, p. 182). In other words, only some of the students in the "DI" group were fully exposed to the program. Neither the printed nor the online report stated separately the results obtained for students with varying levels of exposure or provided details on the mix of programs that was used.

The treatment received by students in the suburban schools was similarly unclear. "DI was implemented as a compensatory model specifically for students who scored low on their first grade screening....Thus, students who received DI in [the district] were exposed to their general education classroom's primary reading curricula...in addition to the DI instruction" (p. 182). The fact that the DI group had many more "lower achieving" students yet had greater average gains and higher scores than the higher achieving students in the control group could be taken as evidence of DI's effectiveness, not its lack of efficacy.

In a letter published in the journal *Education Week* in 2004, DI expert and University of Wisconsin professor Sara Tarver described other problems with the study's design and implementation. Tarver had been asked by DI publisher SRA/McGraw Hill to discuss the proposal with Ryder and his colleagues following the resignation of the project's initial principal investigator. Tarver found that the training that would be given to the Direct Instruction teachers was poorly conceived, incorrectly planned, and hence would render the study an invalid test of Direct Instruction. (See Tarver, S. G. [2004]. February 25. Direct Instruction: Criticism of a Wisconsin study [Letter to the editor]. *Education Week, 23*[24], 38.)

APPENDIX IV:
WHAT DI TEACHERS SAY

Following are actual quotes from teachers using Direct Instruction:

"Direct Instruction does it all. It teaches kids to listen, it teaches kids to think, it teaches kids to respond, it teaches self-control. It does it all. It's hard, but most things that are good are hard."

— Barbara Carroll
Northport, AL

"In all my career with thousands of kids, I've never met a kid who could not learn. And I would not be able to say that without the design of the DI programs."

— Phyllis Haddox
Eugene, OR

"One hundred percent of our children in our classroom reading at grade level is every teacher's dream. And I wasn't getting it until I had this structure. I was always playing catch-up. I haven't seen the child yet that hasn't become successful with DI, whether they've come to school with the background knowledge or not."

— Sunya Lewis
Spring, TX

"DI taught me how to structure tasks so that learning will occur. I'm an engineer in the classroom. That is my job—to be the best engineer possible."

— Maria Collins
Lisle, IL

"DI is the great equalizer."

— Wayne Callender
Boise, ID

"Most teachers spend the whole day throwing out information without really knowing where it landed. With DI you know where it landed."

— *Mary Frances Bruce*
Mathews, AL

"DI was my savior as a teacher. It was a life vest for me. It kept me afloat."

— *Cary Andrews*
Leland, NC

"The reinforcement that the teacher gets with DI is overwhelming. Being able to teach the hardest to teach kids, the amazing technical skills I've gained over the years—that's so empowering."

— *Linda Carnine*
Eugene, OR

"In education you find a lot of people that are incredibly good-hearted and well-intentioned, but they never learn how to teach. I'm a skillful teacher and I attribute it exclusively to DI."

— *Linda Garcia*
Albuquerque, NM

"There is a misperception that DI is hard to teach. Initially it is, but then it's fun because you don't have to worry about kids with holes in their knowledge anymore."

— *Donald Steely*
Eugene, OR

"Teachers worry kids will be bored with DI. It's the opposite—kids love getting the skills. Teachers worry that kids won't work independently, but it's the opposite. DI gives them the skills to be independent. Teachers worry that DI is tracking, that kids in the low track will get a watered down curriculum and move slower. But it's the opposite. DI teaches more efficiently, more intensively, so that you don't have to track. Tracking assumes ability is inborn and you can't do anything about it. DI assumes all kids can learn."

— *Charlotte Andrist*
Columbus, OH

"This is a program that actually can deliver what it promises. It's a life-changing experience for teachers and students. I could never give it up. I'd change jobs and take less money."

— *Linda Youngmayr*
Columbus, OH

"No curriculum allows you to analyze your teaching like Direct Instruction because you're collecting meaningful data all the time that help you plan your lesson for the next day."

— *Sharon Brumbley*
Monroe, OR

"DI provides the structure to allow me to be creative in the classroom. The kids are learning so much faster than you possibly could have taught them without the sequences. I used to spend all this time preparing lesson plans. Now I spend all my time doing the fun stuff."

— *Erin Chaparro*
Eugene, OR

"It's the most exciting, fun successful instruction possible."

— *Don Crawford*
Portland, OR

"DI is designed for diagnostic teaching. Every single thing you put out, you know right away whether they have it or they don't have it."

— *Eileen Cohen*
Atlanta, GA

"You will see changes in your kids within two weeks. Their attention is better. Kids who usually don't speak will speak and answer questions. You see these broken, beat-up kids who don't know anything and are used to being shamed. Their eyes are down, their shoulders are slumped. I've had these kids. It's joyous and fulfilling to watch them change. After one 45-minute lesson, they're on the edge of their seats. That's gold to me."

— *Adrienne Allen*
Columbus, OH

"DI has touched so many people's lives. Troubled kids are leaving institutions and being repatriated with their families, kids are leaving locked facilities for group homes."

> — *Vicky Vachon*
> *Picton, Ontario*

"The scripted lessons give me more time to see what they enjoy and to think about how I'm going to keep them engaged and coming back the next day eager to learn. It's not delivered as a script. It's a conversation with them. I don't feel regimented, I feel like I'm released."

> — *Dorothy Glewwe*
> *Baltimore, MD*

"DI makes kids feel safe and empowered. You're rarely asking them to do anything they're not prepared to do. And they feel safety with unison response."

> — *Karen Galloway*
> *Eugene, OR*

"What faster and more efficient way is there to build their self esteem than to arrange the environment so that they can do something they've never been able to do before and thought they never would be able to do?"

> — *Ray Hall*
> *Tucson, AZ*

"DI is work. But it's not harder work than the other things teachers use, and it works better."

> — *Nancy Woolfson*
> *Eugene, OR*

"It works and you'll know it works by the outcomes along the way. Most teachers really believe what they're doing works and that they have their own evidence to point to. But self perception of effectiveness is not the same as an independent evaluation of effectiveness. DI programs can give you independent ways to evaluate your effectiveness."

> — *Robin Morris*
> *Decatur, GA*

"The main thing DI taught me was there is a difference between being a presenter and a teacher."

— Milly Schrader
Elk Grove, CA

"I learned how to program stimuli to induce learning. That's what Direct Instruction does—it focuses on what is critical to learning: what's crucial to know and how do you focus the learner on that?"

— Ed Sims
Birmingham, AL

"Teacher evaluations are pretty easy using DI. You don't go in and see a dog and pony show. There's no need for that. Our teachers don't get worked up when the principal comes in to do an evaluation. It's like any other day."

— Kathi Sexton
Bel Air, MD

"It's not intuitive, you need training. But once it's in place it's transformational. When it clicks for you, it's totally amazing."

— Jane Carter
Eugene, OR

"No train, no gain—this is not a do it yourself program. The secret is good training up front. If you're not going to train the teachers, don't put in the program. But with a willing administrator, there are no barriers to growth."

— Carolyn Schneider
Travelers Rest, SC

APPENDIX V: ENDNOTES

This book is based on ten years of intermittent research during which the author read the major writings on Direct Instruction; monitored its implementation in twelve schools in the Atlanta Public School system over a three-year period; worked as an education research assistant for APS for three years and then at the Georgia Governor's Office for 18 months; wrote articles about DI and education for the national press; tutored a seven-year-old girl who had been left back in first grade with the DI reading program, Funnix; and interviewed hundreds of people with direct experience in DI, including teachers, teacher aides, students, principals, parents, school superintendents and other district staff, trainers, implementation managers, sales representatives, government officials, program authors, professors and researchers. Appendix VI comprises a representative selection of the people interviewed. All were interviewed for 90 minutes or more, and most were interviewed more than once.

The citations herein represent only a small fraction of the literature on Direct Instruction. The most comprehensive bibliography of Direct Instruction runs more than 100 pages: National Institute for Direct Instruction. (2011). A Bibliography of the Direct Instruction Curriculum and Studies Examining its Efficacy. Eugene, OR: National Institute for Direct Instruction. It lists the DI programs, more than 100 scientific studies of DI's effectiveness (categorized by the type of research design and curricular focus), and a vast range of articles and books related to the theory and research underlying the development of the programs and their implementation. The National Institute for Direct Instruction (NIFDI) also maintains a searchable database of research regarding Direct Instruction: (http://nifdi.org/15/di-research-database).

Page 8

More scientific evidence

Borman, G. D., Hewes, G. M., Overman, L. T., & Brown, S. (2003). Comprehensive school reform and achievement: A meta-analysis. *Review of Educational Research, 73*(2), 125-230.

Hattie, J. A. C. (2009). Visible Learning: A Synthesis of Over 800 Meta-Analyses Relating to Achievement. London, UK: Routledge.

Kennedy, M. M. (1978). *Findings from the Follow Through planned variation study*. Washington DC: U.S. Office of Education.

Stebbins, L. B., St. Pierre, R. G., Proper, E. C., Anderson, R. B., & Cerva, T. R. (1977). *Education as experimentation: A planned variation model* (Vol. IV-A). Cambridge, MA: Abt Associates.

Barely 2% of K-12 teachers
Estimates of the percentage of teachers who use Direct Instruction programs come from interviews with staff at the Association for Direct Instruction, Siegfried Engelmann, and sales representatives from the main publisher of DI programs, SRA/McGraw Hill.

Page 9

A concise description
Engelmann, S., & Colvin, G. (2006). *Rubric for identifying authentic Direct Instruction programs.* Eugene, OR: Engelmann Foundation.

Not by faulty children
Engelmann, S., & Carnine, D. (1991). *Theory of Instruction: Principles and applications.* (Rev. ed., p. 376). Eugene, OR: ADI Press. (First edition published 1982, New York: Irvington)

All 5,000 evaluations
Alessi, G. (1988). Diagnosis diagnosed: A systemic reaction. *Professional School Psychology, 3*(2), 145-151.
Wade, B., & Moore, M. (1993). Experiencing special education: *What young people with special educational needs can tell us.* Buckingham: Open University Press

The study's findings
Alessi, G. (1988). Diagnosis diagnosed: A systemic reaction. *Professional School Psychology, 3*(2), 145-151.

It's the theorists' fault
Unless otherwise attributed, all quotations from Siegfried Engelmann come from personal interviews with the author, conducted between 2001and 2011. The accuracy of the quotes has been confirmed by him.

Page 10

The learning process is the same
Engelmann, S., & Carnine, D. (1991). *Theory of instruction: Principles and applications* (Rev. ed.). Eugene, OR: ADI Press. Engelmann, S., & Carnine, D. (2011). *Could John Stuart Mill have saved our schools?* Verona, WI: Full Court.
Mill, J. S. (1843). *A System of logic, ratiocinative and inductive: Being a connected view of the principles of evidence, and the methods of scientific investigation* (Vol. I). London, UK: John W. Parker.
S. Engelmann (2001-2011). Personal interviews by the author.

Page 11

Wired to do so
Engelmann, S., & Carnine, D. (1991). *Theory of instruction: Principles and applications* (Rev. ed.). Eugene, OR: ADI Press.

54 confirmed the hypothesis
Engelmann, S., & Carnine, D. (1991). *Theory of instruction: Principles and applications* (Rev. ed., Chapters 29-30). Eugene, OR: ADI Press.
Engelmann, S., & Carnine, D. (2011). *Could John Stuart Mill have saved our schools?* Verona, WI: Full Court.

Project Follow Through
Kennedy, M. M. (1978). *Findings from the Follow Through planned variation study.* Washington DC: U.S. Office of Education.

Stebbins, L. B., St. Pierre, R. G., Proper, E. C., Anderson, R. B., & Cerva, T. R. (1977). *Education as experimentation: A planned variation model* (Vol. IV-A). Cambridge, MA: Abt Associates.

Page 12

Project Follow Through chart
Education Consumer Foundation. (2009). *Project Follow Through chart*. Retrieved from www.education-consumers.org/PFT_page.pdf

Page 14

The most revolutionary preschool in America
The facts of Engelmann's biography, including the Bereiter-Engelmann preschool, are gleaned from personal interviews with Engelmann by the author, videos of interviews conducted by others, and print sources cited below.
Engelmann, S. (July 2008.) Conversation with G. Colvin. MPEG4 Recording. 34th Annual Direct Instruction Conference, Eugene, OR. Available from at http://www.zigsite.com
Engelmann, S. (July 2009.) *Theory of Instruction*. Keynote. Presented at the 35th annual National Direct Instruction Conference, Eugene, OR. Available from at http://www.zigsite.com
Engelmann, S. (April 4, 1998). Interview with J. Palfreman. QuickTime Movie. Available from at http://www.zigsite.com
Engelmann, S. (July 5, 2002). Interview with the staff at the National Institute for Direct Instruction. VHS. Title of Event. Available from the National Institute for Direct Instruction. Eugene, OR.
Engelmann, S. (1992). *War against the schools' academic child abuse*. Portland, OR: Halcyon House.
Engelmann, S. (2007). *Teaching needy kids in our backward system: 42 years of trying*. Eugene, OR: ADI Press.
Engelmann, S., & Bereiter, C. (1966). *Teaching disadvantaged children in the preschool*. Engelwood Cliffs, NJ: Prentice-Hall.
Engelmann, S., & Bereiter, C. (1967). An academically oriented preschool for disadvantaged children: Results from the initial experimental group. In D. W. Brison & W. Sullivan (Eds.), *Psychology and early childhood education* (pp. 17–36). Toronto, Ontario, Canada: Ontario Institute for Studies in Education.
Engelmann, S., Bereiter, C., Osborn, J., & Reidford, P. (1966). An academically oriented preschool for culturally deprived children. In F. M. Hechinger (Ed.), *Preschool education today* (pp. 105–136). Garden City, NY: Doubleday.
Tributes to Siegfried Engelmann. Bound volume of 130 tributes from "friends, colleagues, students, protégés, and other admirers" presented to Engelmann July 26, 1994 "on the occasion of the 20th Anniversary of the Eugene Direct Instruction Conference." 161 pages. Unpublished. Made available by the Engelmann-Becker Corp.

Page 15

The largest IQ gains ever recorded
Bereiter, C. & Engelmann, S. (1966). *Effectiveness of Direct Verbal Instruction on IQ performance and achievement in reading and arithmetic*. Champaign, IL: Academic Preschool. Retrieved from ERIC database. (ED030 496) Engelmann, S., & Bereiter, C. (1966). *Teaching disadvantaged children in the preschool*. Engelwood Cliffs, NJ: Prentice-Hall.
Engelmann, S., & Bereiter, C. (1967). An academically oriented preschool for disadvantaged children: Results from the initial experimental group. In D. W. Brison & W. Sullivan (Eds.), *Psychology and early childhood education* (pp. 17–36). Toronto, Ontario, Canada: Ontario Institute for Studies in Education.
Engelmann, S., Bereiter, C., Osborn, J., & Reidford, P. (1966). An academically oriented preschool for culturally deprived children. In F. M. Hechinger (Ed.), *Preschool education today* (pp. 105–136). Garden City, NY: Doubleday.

Results well above the norm
Bissell, J. S. (1973). The cognitive effects of preschool programs for disadvantaged children. In J.L. Frost (Ed.), *Revisiting early childhood education: Readings* (pp. 239-252). New York, NY: Holt, Rinehart, & Winston.

Engelmann, S. (1970). The effectiveness of Direct Instruction on IQ performance and achievement in reading and arithmetic. In J. Hellmuth (Ed.) *Disadvantaged child* (Vol. 3., pp. 339-361). New York, NY: Brunner/Mazel.

Kennedy, M. M. (1978). *Findings from the Follow Through planned variation study.* Washington DC: U.S. Office of Education. Miller, L. B. & Dyer, J. L. (1975). Four preschool programs: Their dimensions and effects. *Monographs of the Society for Research in Child Development, 40* (5-6. Serial No. 162).

Stebbins, L. B., St. Pierre, R. G., Proper, E. C., Anderson, R. B., & Cerva, T. R. (1977). *Education as experimentation: A planned variation model* (Vol. IV-A). Cambridge, MA: Abt Associates.

Weisberg, P. (1988). Direct Instruction in the preschool. *Education and Treatment of Children, 11,* 349-363.

Page 16

Engelmann did it first

Engelmann, S. (1997). *Preventing failure in the primary grades.* Eugene, OR: ADI Press. (Originally published 1969, Chicago: Science Research Associates)

Dixon, R. (1997). Introduction. In S. Engelmann, *Preventing failure in the primary grades* (pp. I-II). Eugene, OR: ADI Press. Dixon elaborated on his observation that "Engelmann did it first" in interviews with the author. Others corroborating Dixon's account in interviews include Barbara Bateman, Russell Gersten, Bonnie Grossen, Robin Morris, Barak Rosenshine, Tim Slocum, and Randy Sprick. (See Appendix VI for identification of interviewed sources.)

The significance of the language gap

Hart, B., & Risley, T. R. (1995). *Meaningful differences in the everyday experience of young American children.* Baltimore, MD: Paul H. Brookes.

Create programs that enabled teachers to close it

Engelmann, S., & Osborn, J. (1998). *Language for learning* (Teacher's Presentation Book, Student Material, and Teacher's Guide). Columbus, OH: SRA/McGraw-Hill.

Stebbins, L. B., St. Pierre, R. G., Proper, E. C., Anderson, R. B., & Cerva, T. R. (1977). *Education as experimentation: A planned variation model* (Vol. IV-A). Cambridge, MA: Abt Associates. Kennedy, M. M. (1978). *Findings from the Follow Through planned variation study.* Washington DC: U.S. Office of Education.

Bissell, J. S. (1973). *The cognitive effects of preschool programs for disadvantaged children.* In J.L. Frost (Ed.), *Revisiting early childhood education: Readings* (pp. 239-252). New York, NY: Holt, Rinehart, & Winston.

The ability to learn math

Ponitz, C., McClelland, M., Matthews, J. S., & Morrison, F. J. (2009, May). A Structured observation of behavioral self-regulation and its contribution to kindergarten outcomes. *Developmental Psychology, 45*(3), 605-19.

Engelmann's first math programs

The Distar Arithmetic programs, first published in 1970, were the first to systematically identify the component skills needed to understand and perform operations with numbers, order the teaching of those skills into a logical sequence of small, manageable tasks, and incorporate frequent feedback and systematic individual practice to insure mastery of the skills—all elements stressed in the subsequent literature on effective math instruction. For example, see pages 48 and 49 of *The Final Report of the National Mathematics Advisory Panel* (US Department of Education, 2008) on the value for low achieving students of "explicit, systematic instruction" and having students "think aloud about the decisions they make when solving problems." See page 47 on the importance of frequent formative assessment (weekly or biweekly) "so that instruction can be adapted based on student progress."

His reading programs anticipated

Engelmann's Distar Reading I-II-III, first published in 1969, anticipated many of the findings from research on reading instruction, including the importance of explicit phonemic instruction, regular assessment of students' growth in skills, and adequate practice to insure fluent wording decoding skills and mastery of new vocabulary. For example, see National Reading Panel, *Teaching children*

73

to read: An evidence-based assessment of the scientific research literature on reading and its implications for reading instruction (NRP, 2000, pp. 2, 7-8, 11-12, and 14). See also the National Research Council report, *Preventing reading difficulties in young children* (NRC, 1998, p. 6). The upper levels of *Reading Mastery* (1983-4), with their heavy emphasis on science, social science and literature, anticipated research showing that reading comprehension depends heavily on general background knowledge. For example, see the National Reading Panel report (NRP, 2000, p. 14), and E. D. Hirsch's *Cultural literacy, what every American needs to know* (1988). The upper and lower level reading programs also use techniques to teach comprehension skills that were later identified as effective by the NRC report (1998, p. 6) and the NRP report (2000, p. 15).

Page 17

Students are more motivated to work hard
For an overview of the research, see Schunk, D. H. (1991). Self-efficacy and academic motivation. *Educational Psychologist, 26*, 207-231.
For a highly-cited study, see Ames, C., & Archer, J. (1988). Achievement goals in the classroom: Students' learning strategies and motivation processes. *Journal of Educational Psychology, 80*, 260-267.
For a review of the larger literature, see Utman, C. H. (1997). Performance effects of motivational state: A meta-analysis. *Personality and Social Psychology Review, 1*, 170-182.

A unique opportunity to help
Reviews of the research regarding changes in brain development that occur with reading can be found in Schlaggar, B. L., & McCandliss, B. D. (2007). Development of neural systems for reading, *Annual Review of Neuroscience, 30*, 475-503; McCandliss, B. D., Cohen, L., & Dehaene, S. (2003). The visual word form area: Expertise for reading in the fusiform gyrus. *Trends in Cognitive Science, 7*, 293-299; Pugh, K. R., Mencl, W. E., Jenner, A. R., Katz, L., Frost, S. J., Lee, J.R., Shaywitz, S.E., and Shaywitz, B. A. (2001). Neurobiological studies of reading and reading disability. *Journal of Communications Disorders, 34*, 479-492.
Examples of studies more directly related to the differential impact on the brain of explicit reading instruction, such as that found in DI, can be found in Aizenstein, H. J., MacDonald, A. W., Stenger, V. A., Nebes, R. D., Larson, J. K., Ursu, S., & Carter, C. S. (2000). Complementary category learning systems identified using event-related functional MRI,. *Journal of Cognitive Neuroscience, 12*, 977-987; Bitan, T., Manor, D., Morocz, I. A., & Karni, A. (2005). Effects of alphabeticality, practice and type of instruction on reading an artificial script: An fMRI study. *Cognitive Brain Research, 25*, 90-106; Buckner, R. L., & Kourtstall, W. (1998). Functional neuroimaging studies of encoding, priming, and explicit memory retrieval. *Proceedings of the National Academy of Science, USA, 95*, 891-898; and Simos, P. G., Fletcher, J. M., Bergman, E., Brier, J. I., Foorman, B. R., Castillo, E. M., Davis, R. N., Fitzgerald, M., & Papanicolaou, A. C. (2002). Dyslexia-specific brain activation profile becomes normal following successful remedial training. *Neurology, 58*, 1203-1213. .

Page 18

The teacher leads the dance
Ehri, L. C., Nunes, S. R., Willows, D. M., Schuster, B. V., Yaghoub-Zadeh, Z., & Shanahan, T. (2001). Phonemic awareness instruction helps children learn to read: Evidence from the National Reading Panel's meta-analysis. *Reading Research Quarterly, 36*, 250–287.
Norris, J. M. & Ortega, L. (2000). Effectiveness of L2 instruction: A research synthesis and quantitative meta-analysis. *Language Learning, 50*, 417-528. Shows superiority of explicit instruction with 2nd language instruction.

Same results with reading
Bangert-Drowns, R. L., & Banker, E. (1990, April). Meta-analysis of effects of explicit instruction for critical thinking. Paper presented at the Annual Meeting of the American Educational Research Association, Boston. Retrieved from ERIC database. (ED 328614)

Same results for critical thinking and mathematics
Baker, S., Gersten, R., & Lee, D. S. (2002). A synthesis of empirical research on teaching mathematics to low-achieving students. *The Elementary School Journal, 103*, 51-73.

The teacher changes the learner
Engelmann, S. (1969). *Conceptual learning* (p. 7). San Rafael, CA: Dimensions.

Page 19

Find a rule
The description of Direct Instruction rules and techniques is the author's synthesis derived from *Theory of Instruction* and personal interviews with Engelmann and several of his co-authors, including Robert Dixon, Owen Engelmann, Bonnie Grossen, Phyllis Haddox, Susie Hanner, Bernadette Kelly, and Jean Osborn. (See Appendix V.)

Engelmann holds up a pencil
The description of Engelmann teaching the principles of instructional design to his students is based on the author's interviews with Engelmann and with many people who were trained by him, including Charlotte Jo Andrist, Linda Carnine, Maria Collins, Margo Fitzgerald, Bonnie Grossen, Phyllis Haddox, Ed Kame'enui, Randy Sprick, Marcy Stein, Vicky Vachon, and Linda Young-mayr. (See Appendix V.)

Page 23

This astonishing language gap
Hart, B., & Risley, T. R. (1995). *Meaningful differences in the everyday experience of young American children.* Baltimore, MD: Paul H. Brookes.

Page 26

Engelmann is meticulous
See endnote 'He tests his programs' (referring to p. 8) above.

Page 27

Testing and teaching become the same package
Engelmann, S., & Carnine, D. (1991). *Theory of instruction: Principles and applications* (Rev. ed.). Eugene, OR: ADI Press.

Page 30

Kids are lawful in what they like
Engelmann, S., & Crawford, D. (2007, Fall). Fixing motivational problems. *Direct Instruction News,* 24-31.

Page 31

The blind hear walls
Cotzin, M., & Dallenbach, K. M. (1950). Facial vision: The role of pitch and loudness in the perception of obstacles by the blind. *American Journal of Psychology, 63,* 485-515.
Hayes, S. P. (1935). Facial vision or the senses of obstacles. Watertown, MA: Perkins.
Supa, M., Cotzin, M., & Dallenbach, K. M. (1944). Facial vision: The perception of obstacles by the blind. *American Journal of Psychology, 62,* 133-183.
Worchel, P., & Dallenbach, K. M. (1947). Perception of obstacles by the deaf-blind. *American Journal of Psychology, 60,* 502-553.

Page 32

The kids never lie
Linda Youngmayr. Interview with the author.

Page 33

At least not obvious

The description of bullet point findings is based on the author's interviews with Engelmann and with his co-authors listed above.

Children with low IQs

Carnine, D., Silbert, J., & Kameenui, E. J. (1990). *Direct instruction reading*. Columbus, OH: Merrill.

Freeman, G. L. (1940). A methodological contribution to nature-nurture dilemma in tested intelligence. *Psychological Review, 47*(3), 267-270.

They do not learn in different ways

Griswold, P. C., Gelzheiser, L. M., & Shepherd, M. J. (1987). Does a production deficiency hypothesis account for vocabulary learning among adolescents with learning disabilities? *Journal of Learning Disabilities, 20*(10), 620-626.

Learning rates change quickly

Eva, K. W., Neville, A. J., & Norman, G. R. (1998). Exploring the etiology of content specificity: Factors influencing analogic transfer and problem solving. *Academic Medicine, 73*(10), S1–S5.

At-risk children don't understand

White, T. G., Graves, M. F., & Slater, W. H. (1990). Growth of reading vocabulary in diverse elementary schools: Decoding and word meaning. *Journal of Educational Psychology, 82*(2), 281-290.

Page 35

Visible Learning

Hattie, J. A. C. (2009). *Visible learning: A synthesis of over 800 meta-analyses relating to achievement*. London, UK: Routledge.

They have learned so much

De Rosa, K. (2009). More Evidence that good instruction can make a big difference. *D'Ed Reckoning*. Retrieved from http://d-edreckoning.blogspot.com/2009/07/more-evidence-that-good-instruction-can.html

De Rosa, K. (2008). Gering public schools: The school district to watch. *D'Ed Reckoning*. Retrieved from http://d-edreckoning.blogspot.com/2008/04/gering-public-schools-school-district.html

De Rosa, K. (2008). Some results out of Gering. *D'Ed Reckoning*. Retrieved from http://d-edreckoning.blogspot.com/2008/04/some-results-out-of-gering.html

De Rosa, K. (2008). More results out of Gering. *D'Ed Reckoning*. Retrieved from http://d-edreckoning.blogspot.com/2008/04/more-results-out-of-gering.html

De Rosa, K. (2008). More Gering data. *D'Ed Reckoning*. Retrieved from http://d-edreckoning.blogspot.com/2008/04/more-gering-data.html

National Institute for Direct Instruction. (2008). The Gering Story video. http://www.nifdi.org/gering_video.html

McEwen, E. (2009). *Teach them all to read*. Thousand Oaks, CA: Corwin.

Elaine McEwen. Interview with the author.

Page 42

17 hours to design a five-minute sequence

The Engelmann protégé was Vicky Vachon, now a project director for the National Institute for Direct Instruction. The information is from an author interview with her.

A System of Logic

Mill, J. S. (1843). A System of Logic, ratiocinative and inductive: Being a connected view of the principles of evidence, and the methods of scientific investigation (Vol. I). London, UK: John W. Parker.

Engelmann, S. & Carnine, D. (2011). *Could John Stuart Mill have saved our schools?* Verona, WI: Full Court.

Page 44

Most of them come around

Bessellieu, F. B., Kozloff, M. A., & Rice, J. S. (2000, Spring). Teachers' perceptions of Direct Instruction teaching. *Direct Instruction News*, 14-18.

Ogletree, E. J., & DiPasalegne, R. W. (1975). Inner-city teachers evaluate DISTAR. *Reading Teacher, 28*, 633-637.

Proctor, T. J. (1989). Attitudes toward Direct Instruction. *Teacher Education and Special Education, 12*, 40-45.

Schug, T., Tarver, S., & Western, R. (2001). Direct Instruction and the teaching of early reading. *Wisconsin Policy Research Institute Report, 14*, 1-29

Page 46

A missile in flight

The stories of Engelmann's achievements working with children, in this chapter and elsewhere, are drawn from author interviews with people who witnessed them, including Adrienne Allen, Muriel Berkeley, Elaine Bruner, Linda Carnine, Maria Collins, Don Crawford, Gary Davis, Robert Dixon, Kurt and Owen Engelmann, Bonnie Grossen, Phyllis Haddox, Susie Hanner, Martin Kozloff, Sam Miller, Jean Osborn, Jerry Silbert, and Linda Youngmayr. The stories have been confirmed by Engelmann.

Bet anyone $100,000

The story of Engelmann's bet is from an author interview with him and is corroborated by author interviews with several of his colleagues, including Robert Dixon, Jerry Silbert, and Vicky Vachon.

Page 47

A special breed

The characterization of DI teachers is based on author interviews with more than 40 teachers. See Appendix IV and VI for a selection of quotations and names.

Appendix I

The account is based on a site visit by the author in May 2008 to Stephanie Brown's class, and the author's interview with her after the class.

APPENDIX VI:
LIST OF SOURCE INTERVIEWS

The author formally interviewed the following people between 2008 and 2011 for *Clear Teaching*. The author also had frequent conversations with many of the same people for other projects related to Direct Instruction between 2001 and 2008. Identifications reflect each person's status at the time of the interview.

Dr. Gary Adams
Co-author, *Research on Direct Instruction: 25 Years Beyond DISTAR*
Portland, OR

Grace Adams
Parent of child who attended DI childcare center
Tuscaloosa, Alabama

Anayezuka Ahidiana
DI trainer and consultant
Baltimore, MD

*+Adrienne Allen
DI trainer
Columbus, OH

Cary Andrews
Assoc. Supt. of Instruction, Roger Bacon Charter Schools
Leland, NC

+Charlotte Giovanetti Andrist
Education consultant, Associate Professor and Director, Reading Clinic, Notre Dame College
Cleveland, OH

Jennifer Ashlock
President, Ashlock Consulting Inc.
Petaluma, CA

Lynann Barbero
Director of Special Education, Reading First Supervisor, Bureau of Indian Affairs
New Legacy Partnerships
Santa Fe, NM

Barbara Bateman
Professor Emerita, University of Oregon
Eugene, OR

Muriel Berkeley
Executive Director, Baltimore Curriculum Project
Baltimore, MD

Frances Bessellieu
National Consultant, Side-by-Side K-12 Consulting Services
Wilmington, NC

Molly Blakely
President, Educational Resources Inc.
Missoula, MT

Lindsay Boorman
Esq. VP of Operations, JP Associates
Valley Stream, NY

Maggie Boozer
School Improvement Specialist, JP Associates
Valley Stream, NY

Sharon Brumbley
Special education teacher
Monroe, OR

Louise Bronaugh
CEO, BEST Workshops for Educators
Eugene, OR

Mary Frances Bruce
Retired DI teacher
Mathews, AL

*+Elaine Bruner
DI trainer
Urbana, IL

Wayne Callender
President, Partners for Learning
Regional Educational Coordinator, University of Oregon
Boise, Idaho

*+Doug Carnine
Co-author, *Theory of Instruction*
Eugene, OR

*+Linda Carnine
DI trainer, co-author, Corrective Reading
Eugene, OR

Barbara Carroll
Retired DI teacher
Northport, AL

Jane Carter
Principal, Spring Creek Elementary School
Eugene, OR

Erin Chaparro
Research Associate, University of Oregon
Eugene, OR

Eileen Cohen
Cognitive Development Specialist, Georgia State University
Atlanta, GA

Maria Collins
DI trainer
Lisle, IL

Geoff Colvin
Educational Consultant, Behavior Associates
Eugene OR

Don Crawford
Executive Director, Mastery Learning Institute, Arthur Academy
Portland, OR

Kelli Cummings
Research Associate, University of Oregon
Eugene, OR

Karen Galloway
Title I Teacher Coordinator, Spring Creek Elementary School
Eugene, OR

Mary Damer
Partner, Multi-Tier LL Consulting
Columbus, OH

*+Gary Davis
National Coordinator & Project Director, National Institute for Direct Instruction (NIFDI)
Eugene, OR

+Karen Lou Seitz Davis
DI first-grade teacher
Eugene, OR

*Bob Dixon
Author, *Reading Success, DI spelling programs*
Olympia, WA

Laura Doherty
Project Director, NIFDI
Baltimore, MD

Donald Doran
Principal, Drew Charter School, Atlanta Public Schools
Atlanta, GA

Kurt Engelmann
President, National Institute for Direct Instruction
Eugene, OR

Owen Engelmann
Director of Curricular Resources, NIFDI
Eugene, OR

*Siegfried Engelmann
Eugene, OR

Therese Engelmann
Eugene, OR

+Janie Feinberg
President, JP Associates
Valley Stream, NY

Janet Fender
Founder, My Direct Instruction Consultant LLC
Hockessin, DE

Karen Fierman
Engelman-Becker Corp.
Eugene, OR

+Margo Fitzgerald
Retired DI preschool teacher and coordinator
Seattle, WA

+Linda Garcia
Retired DI trainer
Albuquerque, NM

Russ Gersten
Professor Emeritus, University of Oregon
Executive Director, Instructional Research Group
Los Alamitos, CA

Mary Gleason
DI trainer, Co-author, REWARDS Program
Eugene, OR

Dorothy Glewwe
Kindergarten teacher, City Springs Elementary School
Baltimore, MD

Roland Good III
Associate Professor, School Psychology, University of Oregon
Creator of DIBELS
Eugene, OR

+Alex Granzin
School Psychologist, Springfield Public Schools
Springfield, OR

*+Bonnie Grossen
Executive Director, Center for Applied Research in Education, University of Oregon
Hillsboro, OR

*+Phyllis Haddox
Co-author, *Teach Your Child to Read in 100 Easy Lessons*
Retired professor, University of Oregon
Eugene, OR

Ray Hall
Implementation Manager, NIFDI
Tucson, AZ

*+Susie Hanner
Co-author, Reading Mastery
Eugene, OR

Eric Irizarry
Assistant Headmaster, Charter Day School
Leland, NC

Ed Kame'enui
Associate Dean for Research and Outreach, Director, Center on Teaching and Learning
University of Oregon

Bernadette Kelly
Co-author, *Essentials for Algebra, Connecting Math Concepts*
Pacific City, OR

Martin Kozloff
Professor, University of North Carolina Wilmington
Wilmington, NC

Nadine Kujawa
Retired Superintendent, Aldine Independent School District and Executive Director, Rodeo Institute for Teacher Excellence
Houston, TX

Sunya Lewis
Assistant Director, Rodeo Institute for Teacher Excellence
Spring, TX

John Wills Lloyd
Professor, University of Virginia
Charlottesville, VA

Elaine McEwan-Adkins
McEwan-Adkins Group
Author, Teach Them ALL to Read
Oro Valley, AZ

Samuel Miller
Retired K-12 teacher/education consultant, co-author, *Cursive Writing*
Eugene, OR

+Carol Morimitsu
Retired DI trainer
Chicago, IL

Robin Morris
Associate Provost for Strategic Initiatives & Innovation, Georgia State University
Atlanta, GA

Emily Osborn
Assistant Professor of African History, University of Chicago
Chicago, IL

*+Jean Osborn
Associate Director, Center for the Study of Reading, University of Illinois
Co-author, *Language for Learning, Language for Thinking, Language for Writing*
Champaign, IL

Gloria Patterson
Executive Director SRT-3, Atlanta Public Schools
Atlanta, GA

Barak Rosenshine
Professor Emeritus, University of Illinois at Champaign-Urbana
Champaign, IL

*Ed Schaefer
Vice President, Education Resources Inc.
Missoula, MT

*Carolyn Schneider
Education Consultant
Travelers Rest, SC

*+Milly Schrader
Retired principal, Elk Grove Unified School District, DI trainer
Elk Grove, CA

Kathryn Sexton
Curriculum Coordinator, Hampstead Hill Academy
Bel Air, MD

*+Jerry Silbert
DI trainer, Engelmann-Becker Corp.
Eugene, OR

Ed Sims
Retired DI preschool teacher/trainer, Early Childhood Day Care Center, University of Alabama
Birmingham, AL

Tim Slocum
Professor, Utah State University
Logan, UT

Terry Smith
Executive Director, Proviso Area for Exceptional Children
Maywood, IL

Marilyn Sprick
President, Pacific Northwest Publishing
Eugene, OR

*+Randy Sprick
Educational Consultant, Safe & Civil Schools
Eugene, OR

*+Donald Steely
Co-author, *Inferred Functions of Performance and Learning*
Eugene, OR

*+Marcy Stein
Professor, University of Washington Tacoma
Tacoma, WA

Jean Stockard
Director of Research, NIFDI
Eugene, OR

Vicky Vachon
Project Director, NIFDI
Picton, Ontario, Canada

Jason Vancura
Autistic student taught with DI (interviewed by email)
Worth, IL

Maria Vanoni
DI trainer
Stony Brook, NY

Linda Vinson
Vice President of Sales, Mid-Atlantic Region, SRA/McGraw-Hill Education K-8
Franklin, TN

Paul Weisberg
Professor Emeritus, University of Alabama
Director, Early Childhood Day Care Center
Tuscaloosa, AL

Roberta Weisberg
Teacher and administrator, Tuscaloosa City Schools
Tuscaloosa, AL

Nancy Woolfson
DI teacher and trainer
Eugene, OR

*+Linda Youngmayr
Special Education teacher and DI Trainer
Columbus, OH

* Association for Direct Instruction Hall of Fame member. ADI, a non-profit membership organization, has inducted 24 people into its Hall of Fame since the Hall's inception in 1999.

+ Participated in the training, monitoring and/or analysis of schools implementing DI in the federal government's Follow Through project, the largest study in history to compare different approaches to instruction.

To Receive Additional Copies of This Book

Clear Teaching is available in electronic (PDF) format at no cost from the Education Consumers Foundation's website. You can download your copy at **www.education-consumers.org**. Note that this book may be freely distributed as long as copyright and author information are included.

Printed copies are available individually for $15.95 plus shipping from the Foundation and from other sources. For information on bulk purchases, please contact the Foundation at ecf@education-consumers.org.